COMING HOME

WALES AFTER THE WAR

PHIL CARRADICE

D1387132

Gomer

First Impression – 2005

ISBN 1 84323 476 9

This book is published with the financial
support of the Welsh Books Council.

Printed in Wales at
Gomer Press, Llandysul, Ceredigion

Contents

Acknowledgements

As a child of the post-war period – I was born in 1947, one of the 'baby boomers' as they call us – the first acknowledgement has to be to my mother and father. Without the Second World War they would never have met and I would not be here. I make no apologies for quoting both of them in this book, having interviewed them shortly before their deaths: their contributions are as valid and as fascinating as any of the others. The fact that they were related to the author is, frankly, incidental.

Thanks also to all of the other people I interviewed in the course of my research. Without them, without their wholehearted responses to my questions, the book would not have been possible.

Most of the illustrative material in this book was provided by the individuals who gave so willingly of their time. They are personal photographs that provide a fascinating glimpse of life in the 1940s. To everyone who contributed, many thanks. Several photographs and source materials come from the author's own collection. Other thanks go to: Merthyr Tydfil Libraries for the wonderful photographs of street parties at the end of the war and queues; George Best for his photograph of Penarth County School; Ivy Davies for the Souvenir Programme of the Llantwit Major peace celebrations and Richard Phillips for his photographs of prefab life.

Finally – and as always – to Trudy, my wife, who typed the manuscript. Without her it would have been an impossible task.

Introduction

VE Day was celebrated on 8th May, 1945, technically marking the beginning of what is now called the 'post-war period.' Everyone had known the war was as good as over four days earlier, however, when representatives of the German army surrendered to Field Marshal Montgomery at Luneburg Heath.

Despite that surrender, sporadic fighting continued for a short while, particularly around the city of Salzburg. As late as 7th May, the very day that Dwight Eisenhower watched General Jodl sign formal documents of unconditional surrender, the final U-boat kill of the war took place off the coast of Scotland. Herman Goering and other Nazi leaders were soon captured and when, on 11th May, the last remnants of the German Army Group Centre capitulated to the Russians, the fighting in Europe was finally over.

The war in the East was to continue for another three months, the Japanese surrender coming only after two atomic bomb attacks on Hiroshima and Nagasaki in early August. The attacks – and the subsequent Japanese surrender – came as a great surprise, as much to the military as the ordinary people. The war against Japan had been confidently expected to last well into 1946, perhaps even into 1947, involving a costly and brutal assault on the Japanese homeland, with the prospect of thousands of American, British and colonial casualties.

VJ Day – Victory over Japan Day – was duly celebrated on 15th August. When General MacArthur accepted the Japanese surrender on board USS Missouri on 2nd September, the Second World War officially came to a close. It had lasted six years and one day, affecting the lives of people in over 200 different countries. Millions of servicemen and civilians had died in the conflict but to the relief of the whole world, the war was now, finally, at an end.

With the days of destruction over, people could look to the future with hope and expectation. It was a time of reconstruction – of cities and towns, of industry and commerce and, above all, of individual dreams. The men and women of the armed forces could now think about going home and picking up the pieces of their stranded, disordered lives. For the civilians – the wives and parents and partners who had waited – the shrouds of worry and concern that had lain across their hopes for so long were finally lifted.

It took some getting used to. When, on VE Day – Victory in Europe Day – a thunderstorm had broken out over the city of London it sounded as if the German bombers had returned once more. As Peter Hennessy has said, however,

> For the first time in five and a half years the inhabitants . . . knew it wasn't yet another aerial attack. Acquired reactions and habits could, at last, be shed.
>
> (*Never Again* Peter Hennessy)

For some the readjustment to civilian life and a world at peace would be relatively simple. For many more it would take years for them to truly adapt. And for those who had lost sons and daughters, partners and loved ones, the pain would never go away.

The people of Wales, like people in every other country that had been in any way touched by the conflict, had to come to terms with what was, effectively, a new world. They looked back on the pre-war days, the 1930s, as a time of depression and unemployment. It had been what the poet W H Auden called 'A low, dishonest decade.'

In 1945 the post-war period beckoned. It was a new beginning, the start of a golden era. The people of Britain had fought the war in order to create a better world – now they would reap the harvest that had cost so much. The excitement was tangible.

Soldiers from the barracks in Brecon found themselves celebrating the news of Germany's surrender in nearby Merthyr Tydfil. This photograph shows soldiers and locals on the day peace was declared. Notice the message chalked up on the wall – 'Victory'.

Chapter One

It's Over

V Day marked the end of nearly six years of war and newspapers like the *News Chronicle* were jubilant in their celebrations.

FOR MOST of the people in Britain, Wales included, the war in Europe had been their immediate concern. It was understandable. The battles in France, Belgium and Germany had taken place close at hand and names like Normandy, Arnhem and Berlin were, by 1945, familiar to everyone. But India and Burma? They were far away, part of a distant Empire, not quite a secondary concern but somewhere that did not really bother most people – unless, of course, they had relatives who were serving in those far-off countries.

Apart from anything else, the war had, perhaps for the first time, impinged itself directly on the civilian population of Britain. And it had done so in a particularly cruel and bitter fashion. Over 500,000 houses had been destroyed by aerial bombardment during the conflict and 50,000 civilians killed. Welsh cities and towns had suffered, Swansea being pulverised by German bombers in the three-day blitz of 1941. Smaller towns like Pembroke Dock and Cwmparc, near Treorchy, had also been badly hit.

So it was understandable that news of Germany's surrender brought an immediate and joyous outpouring of emotion. To many it felt as if a dam or a wall had been broken down and all the pent-up fear and anger of the previous six years was simply swept away.

In London the crowds poured onto the streets in their thousands, singing and dancing their way up the Mall towards Buckingham Palace. But in Welsh towns, too, there were immediate and spontaneous celebrations.

MARCO CARINI was, at the time, a young boy in Beaufort and he remembers his excitement at hearing the news.

MARCO CARINI

> We were out the back and, at the end of our street, there was a man with a wireless. He came running out into the yard – 'We've won the war!' he shouted, 'We've won the war! They've surrendered, Germany's surrendered. It's victory, victory!'
>
> And the three of us, we just ran up and down the back road, shouting at everybody to come out, telling them it was all over – because, you see, a lot of people didn't have a wireless then.
>
> By the time we got down to the old Post Office, down the road, most of the other boys in the town were coming up the hill towards us. They were doing the same as us. We were all shouting 'The war's over, the war's over!'
>
> We were elated, all us kids. I don't suppose we really knew what was going on. We were just making a noise. But, oh, the excitement!

For many civilians, adults and children alike, there were mixed reactions to the news. ESTELLE CLARKE and SYLVIA BAILEY looked at things with very different eyes.

ESTELLE CLARKE

> When the war in Europe ended, my husband was still fighting out in Burma. So we didn't have much to celebrate. I'm afraid it was just a glass of mother's home-made wine and then off to bed. But, when Bob came home after VJ night, that was our real celebration.

SYLVIA BAILEY

> I can remember everyone being so joyful, so happy. People were running out into the streets. It's quite vivid in my mind. We lit bonfires! And the tarmac sort of melted away because there wasn't just one bonfire in the road, you'd find three or four all along the street!

The lighting of bonfires had a significance that almost bordered on the spiritual. Although the blackout had been reduced to a 'dim out' in September 1944, lighting fires and showing bright lights remained illegal. So to celebrate with a huge bonfire was a chance not to be missed!

Right across Wales the flames of hundreds of sudden fires leapt high into the night skies – skies that, until relatively recently, had brought only death and destruction. *The Merthyr Express* for 25th August, 1945, summed up the effect:

> Bonfires were lit in the streets and on the mountain-side, and in many cases throughout the Borough the fires which burned on tarmacadam roads have left telltale black scars.

For children in rural areas the ability to light a bonfire was a pleasure that was almost beyond description. EILUNED REES was a child in Llansteffan at the time.

EILUNED REES
> I remember the celebrations. We had a bonfire. When you think that most of what I remembered in my life up till then was blackout, to have a bonfire was fantastic. I don't think there were fireworks and I don't remember there being anything to eat. I think we were just there, with the bonfire.

The celebrations continued late into the night, relief and pleasure fuelling the wild excitement of the moment.

MARCO CARINI
> That night most of the children in town had gone to bed. We were in my parents' shop until it shut at 10.00 p.m. Then Beaufort was lined with people all shouting, having a party in the main street – just happy to be outside. My younger brother and I were leaning out through the bedroom window, looking at it all. There were American soldiers – their camp wasn't all that far away. And all the prisoners, the Italian POWs from the nearby camp at Crickhowell, they were let out, too. They were all there, in the street.

For most people serving in the armed forces there was an immediate feeling of relief. The war was over and, although it might take time, they knew that sooner or later they would be going home. Nearly five million men had served in the forces during the war, nineteen per cent of the male population of the UK. Shortly after VE Day, Ernest Bevin, the Minister of Labour and National Service, announced that release from military service would begin by 18th June. It was hoped to have at least 750,000 people back in civilian life by the end of the year. For some – newly released prisoners of war, for example – returning home came sooner than they had ever imagined. The late CHARLIE STERRY was freed by advancing American forces early in 1945.

CHARLIE STERRY
> They put us in Dakotas and flew us to Brussels. Then they put us into Lancaster bombers and we flew to an airfield in Beaconsfield. We went into a big hanger, where they deloused us, gave us new clothes and a couple of

pounds. 'Go home' they said and so I caught a train to Newport. And that was it, I was out.

For most servicemen and servicewomen, however, it was a case of 'wait your turn.' First in, first out was the general rule. For the moment all they could do was celebrate the end of hostilities – and in some cases that was hard to do, as GLYN MILLER recalls:

GLYN MILLER

I can't remember VE Day at all. I was on the Burma front, with the 14th Army and we were still fighting then. I remember hearing, a day or two after it happened, about the atom bombs being dropped. That was the day I had a tooth taken out – by a Medical Officer, not a dentist! That was the last time I ever had a tooth out.

I don't remember much celebration. We had a Sergeant's Mess, of course. It was a bamboo hut with a grass roof. And for the first time we were allowed a bottle of spirits – in fact we were allowed two. I had a bottle of Booth's Gin and a bottle of VAT 69. That was our celebration.

The late JACK CARRADICE was interviewed shortly before his death. He was a Staff Sergeant in the REME in the Far East when the war ended.

JACK CARRADICE

How did I feel? Flat, I suppose – both times. The first time, VE Day, we heard the news and we

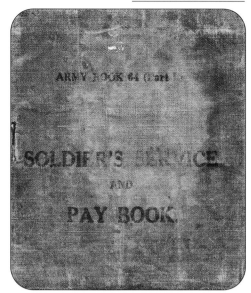

A Soldier's Service and Pay Book, an important document as demob usually took place on a 'first in, first out' basis.

Glyn Miller, in Calcutta, January 1946 – waiting to be sent home.

thought 'Fair enough, that's finished off old Hitler but we're still out here, fighting the bloody Japanese.' And we knew they wouldn't give up easily. We knew we'd have to invade their islands and that a lot of us would probably be dead before it was finished. That's what made you sad: to think you'd come this far and that you might still get killed.

When the news came that they'd dropped the bomb, that the Japs were asking for peace, I was down in the south of India. My unit was part of the planned invasion force, getting ready for the final attack. So, suddenly, you find out that it was all over – and you just felt hollow. Happy, safe, but hollow. It was all over, that was all there was to it.

For many people on the Home Front it was a case of carrying on with life, particularly for those like HUBERT 'BUZZER' REYNOLDS, who was in the fire service at the time. On VE Day he was detailed to pick up an official from the Home Office who was coming to visit the town.

HUBERT 'BUZZER' REYNOLDS

I was stationed at Pontypridd and came down to Cardiff to pick up this man – Mr Munro, I think it was – and another colleague from the Home Office. I was in a big Humber, a left-hand drive – you just used any car you could get in those days.

Anyway I picked this chap up at Cardiff station and brought him back to Pontypridd. And he enjoyed himself, walking around, talking to all the people. I don't know what it was all about but it was funny to have someone come down from London just to walk about like that. That was my VE Day.

JOAN MACDONALD was in the Women's Land Army during the war.

JOAN MACDONALD

I finished the war at Sir Cennydd and Lady Traherne's home, as herdswoman to their beautiful herd of pedigree Guernseys. They were housed in a very modern farm and dairy.

When VE Day came along, all of the Land Army girls went into Cardiff and just danced and danced for hours. We were all so happy. Then, at the end of the night, we took taxis back to the farm. Next day it was back to work, as normal.

For Bevin Boys like HARVEY ALFORD, working in the mines rather than serving in the forces, it was also a case of business as normal.

HARVEY ALFORD

At the end of the war in Europe, I was in a big open-air party near Lewistown, shouting and singing and scoffing free teas and cakes and buns. Everyone was pretty chuffed with themselves and I thought 'Well, I'll be going home now.'

But I didn't. I had to stay in the mines until 1947. It was first in, first out and I hadn't been called up until 1944. I suppose I could have picked up my goods and gone home. But carry on until the bitter end, that's me.

People who followed the progress of the war in Europe in their newspapers or on the radio were aware that the end was coming but in some instances there was an even clearer indication. JOAN SMITH explains:

JOAN SMITH

An uncle of mine worked in the Royal Mews. He'd been called up and went on to become a Regimental Sergeant Major. His wife, my aunt, went back to Cresselly in Pembrokeshire with their two children.

He'd been postilion to the Queen and was in charge of the horses so he was brought back home from the army to get the horses back up to scratch, ready for the celebrations.

He was back early so everyone in Cresselly knew that the war was ending – the war in Europe, anyway.

For some servicemen and servicewomen there was an immediate dilemma once peace arrived. For others there was no doubt about what they wanted to happen. BARBARA JONES was in the WRNS, MARY PHILLIPS in the WAAF:

BARBARA JONES

I had mixed feelings at the end of the war. My friend and I – we'd been friends from the beginning – had signed up for training with Fleet Mail because more and more categories were opening up after the war had finished. But then, at the last minute, she got homesick and wanted to come out. I decided I wouldn't go on without her. So I just took my demob. I often wished I'd stayed in – but there we are.

MARY PHILLIPS

I couldn't wait to come out. I'd had some good times and it was okay when I was close to home. But then they posted me to Honiton and I wasn't very happy there. So when the chance came I got out.

BARBARA JONES

I can't say I really minded coming out. You took things as they came then. You'd just do what you had to do and think afterwards.

JACK CARRADICE

I had the chance to go for a commission and stay in. And I must admit I did think about it for a while. But after six years of being ordered about, of being pushed from pillar to post, there wasn't much of a decision to be made. A lot of blokes had the same choice – most of them decided to come out.

Staff Sergeant Jack Carradice (front left), a photograph taken just before demob.

A small minority decided to remain in the armed forces, individuals who had particularly enjoyed their period of service. The vast majority, however, were only too pleased to be free and away from army discipline.

They weren't professional soldiers – although many had achieved high professional standards during their service – and were clearly aware that they had signed on for the duration only. Now the hills and valleys of Wales beckoned.

JACK CARRADICE

I'd met Mary, my future wife, in 1940, soon after I came back from Dunkirk and my unit was posted to Pembrokeshire. Then I was sent off to India and after that our courtship – if that's what you call it – was by letter.

So I wanted out, I wanted to see her, to settle down to a normal life. The army? You could forget it.

In Wales, in the houses and homes of serving soldiers, it wasn't a case of wondering whether or not loved ones would stay in the army or navy or air force. It was, rather, a matter of wondering how soon they would be home. Every conceivable mode of transport was used to get soldiers back home after the war and even aircraft carriers were pressed into the service of transporting men rather than machines. It took time, however, to get people home and in the meantime there was celebrating to be done.

Parties and all manner of official events to celebrate the end of the war were quickly organised, over and above the spontaneous outpourings of good fellowship that occurred as soon as the news got out. They took place as soon as possible after VE and VJ Days but in some cases the official celebrations were held as late as twelve or even eighteen months after the end of the war. In some instances these were very grand affairs. For people like SYLVIA BAILEY, JOAN SMITH and HARRY RADCLIFFE the celebrations are hard to forget.

SYLVIA BAILEY

> There were fancy-dress parties, concerts, all sorts of things. People were so happy to be out and about after living, sort of, behind closed doors. It had been so quiet during the war and then, suddenly, it was alive again.

JOAN SMITH

> I was living in Pembroke when the war ended. The celebrations were, I think, mostly held in the castle where there was a big green where everybody was dancing. Everyone was there and there were spotlights and everything. Dancing, music, fireworks – all that type of thing.

HARRY RADCLIFFE

> VE night was one of the most spectacular things in the valley. All of Nantymoel – and Ogmore Vale – were out in the streets, dancing and singing until the early hours of the morning.

JOAN SMITH

> There were official celebrations for both VE and VJ days. It's funny but we were quite confident we'd soon wipe out the Japs. Once the one war was over, we thought the other one wouldn't be long.
>
> Pembroke was a garrison town and troops were coming and going all the time. All through my childhood we woke to the sound of the bugle in the morning.

A street party to celebrate the end of the war in Alma Street, Merthyr Tydfil – everyone chipped in to provide the food and drink.

A formal photograph taken during victory celebrations in 1945.

And I remember, being in a shop one day, still feeling that the war against the Japanese would soon be over. It was half full of these soldiers, buying cigarettes and things. They went out and a woman said 'Poor things, they're on embarkation leave. They haven't got time to go home so they're staying in town. Poor things, half of them won't be coming back.'

You couldn't believe it, really. They were only young, in their late teens, early twenties. They were going off to fight the Japanese. It really brought it home to me.

BARBARA JONES was in Plymouth when a huge Victory party was held. The WRNS, like other service units, took part in the celebrations.

BARBARA JONES

They had this big V Parade – they had them all over the country. We were taken in to some spot and had to wait for ages before we were lined up. The navy, of course, was always first in the parade. You'd have the Marine Band and then the sailors and then the WRNS. But somehow we had the American Navy Band behind us and they were very jazzy. In front we had the Marines. We weren't the best of marchers to start with but between those two bands we didn't know which foot to put forward. It must have been the worst marching ever seen, some of us concentrating on the Marine Band, some concentrating on the Americans.

For some children, like VALERIE CARINI, however, the Victory party was something of a damp squib. She was just four years old at the time, living in Beaufort.

VALERIE CARINI

They had a party, almost outside my house. They painted a big V on the wall but I'd cut my tongue. I was bleeding a lot and I couldn't go to the party because I was home from school. My teeth had gone through the end of my tongue. Everyone else went to the party but I had to stay home.

The one thing that most people recall about the end of the war was the lifting of blackout regulations. HARRY RADCLIFFE, EILUNED REES and DILYS CHAPMAN remember it well.

HARRY RADCLIFFE

VE night – the lights go on again! That was the wonderful thing. Street lights were on, house lights were on. There wasn't so much electric light then, it was mostly gas, but seeing it told us that it was all over at last.

EILUNED REES

Nowadays it's very difficult for people to imagine what total blackness is like. You've got so much light pollution now, you never see total blackness. We had total blackness. Unless there was a moon you could see nothing, nothing whatsoever.

Your eyes adapted remarkably well but it was very nice to see all the lights in people's houses. When I was a student, years later, and going out for a walk with a boyfriend on a Saturday night, he used to be very put out by the fact that I loved looking into people's front rooms through the lighted windows. I don't think he realized what this meant to somebody who'd been brought up during the war and had never seen it.

DILYS CHAPMAN

You didn't realize at the time. Day after day, you were getting up in the dark. Everything was dark. You had to keep the lights out, curtains drawn. And then it was just as if something was lifted. The lights went on again. It was great.

HARRY RADCLIFFE

Up until VE Day we'd had the blackout. You'd come home from work and everything would be in darkness. You couldn't see a thing. You had to struggle to walk home – or to go to work if you were working nights.

And it wasn't just the blackout. There were other changes to people's lives, changes that were eagerly embraced and welcomed.

EILUNED REES

Suddenly we could go to every part of the beach again because they took away the barbed wire. And in the summer they had the ferries once more – the ferry to Laugharne and the other ferry to Ferryside. They were just rowing boats, with a sail if the weather was right, and they were really for the holidaymakers. But it was great fun to be able to cross on the ferries again.

For EILUNED REES one of the most wonderful changes to come once the war ended was the ringing of church bells – on the face of it a simple enough practice but something that had been outlawed during the war years when it was deemed that church bells were only to be rung in the event of invasion.

EILUNED REES

Suddenly to hear the ringing of the church bells – it was great. I wasn't a church-goer, I went to chapel. But it was lovely hearing the bells again in the village. I suppose it was a sort of continuation.

The bells had been rung for centuries. They were so much part of village life. Perhaps not so much now but they were at that time. And to hear the bells again – well, it was like ringing in a new age.

For JOAN SMITH the most noticeable change was that people in her town began to actually work on their houses once more.

JOAN SMITH

During the war people had done nothing to their houses, because of the bombing and things. It was a sheer waste of time. For five years houses were untouched. And then they all started to do their places up. They couldn't get wallpaper, then, so they stripped the walls and emulsioned or painted them. I actually remember emulsion coming in: it would be pale blue or green. Everybody brightened everything up at that time.

Above all there was a change of government. Despite the fact that the Conservative Party had won the last pre-war election, throughout the war years from May 1940 onwards, Winston Churchill had led a war cabinet drawn from all political parties. In effect it was a Coalition Government. Once Hitler and Germany were defeated, that state of affairs could not last long. Indeed, Churchill had begun discussions with his deputy Anthony Eden about a possible election date within days of the German surrender. Churchill himself wanted to delay any such vote until June but, while an opinion poll of 1944 suggested that the majority of British voters would like the Coalition to continue, the Labour Party was almost totally opposed to its continuation.

Clement Atlee, leader of the Labour Party, informed Churchill on 21st May that he and his colleagues could not lay aside their political differences any longer. In his words 'the expectation of an election has engaged the attention of the country.'

The result of the election – the 'khaki election' as it is sometimes known – was delayed until 26th July, 1945, as time was needed to gather in and count the votes of the British servicemen from various theatres of war across the world. When those votes were counted, it amounted to a landslide victory by 146 seats for Atlee's Labour Party. They had campaigned on a 'never again' ticket with public ownership of industries like mining, steel production and the railways as the central facet of their manifesto. And the vote of the armed forces was a significant factor in the result.

Serving soldiers like JACK CARRADICE and GLYN MILLER were keen to cast their votes.

JACK CARRADICE

It wasn't an anti-Churchill vote. There was a lot of good-natured sentiment around for the old bloke. People remembered what he'd said and done, what he'd represented during the Blitz. But we'd spent years being told what to do, being ordered about in the army – and before, come to that. This was our chance to hit back, to tell people what we wanted for a change.

Churchill and the Tories? Well, they represented everything that was old world– the 1930s, our war service, everything. We wanted a new world – we'd fought for it – and voting for Labour was a good way to start.

GLYN MILLER

As far as I remember, it was just an ordinary vote, a postal vote. You put your cross on a piece of paper and it was sent off. We had an Army-Based Post Office with us – bear in mind we were in a forward position at that time, in the jungle – and the votes were taken back to base and sent off.

JACK CARRADICE

I suppose we were all a bit fed up with the army bullshit – that's the only way to describe it. We'd been getting it for years and we hadn't been able to do anything about it, up till now.

You've got to remember, I was only 18 when the war began. I was just 19 when I was sitting on the beach at Dunkirk, wondering if I was going to be lifted off or taken prisoner. By the age of 21, I was out in India and Burma – and the culture shock of that, the people and the smells, that awful wasteland of amazing but beautiful places, it was bound to influence you, wasn't it?

So the election of 1945? I don't think Churchill had a chance. It was a reaction – we were going to get rid of the bullshit they'd fed us for years. And by God, we did!

The meal is over, now the organisers can sit down and relax – and have their photographs taken. This photograph was snapped during VJ celebrations in Argyle Street, Twynrodyn.

G̲LYN̲ M̲ILLER̲

   It wasn't an anti-Churchill vote but it may have been an anti-establishment
   one. I guess it was a reaction to everything we'd had to endure.

   I suppose the result was a bit of a shock although everybody I knew voted
   for Labour – so maybe it shouldn't have been. There was a lot of – I don't
   know what you'd call it – revolutionary feeling about. After the war had
   finished out in the east, I was in an open-air cinema up in Assam and there was
   a group of British soldiers shouting out really left wing – communist, I
   suppose – slogans. There weren't many of them but they were pretty vocal. I
   remember it shocked me a bit at the time.

The mood at home was equally euphoric. Miners like HARRY RADCLIFFE and
young men such as JOHN PULLEY remember the time with great clarity.

H̲ARRY̲ R̲ADCLIFFE̲

   Oh, it was everything, the election of 1945! We thought we were going to have
   a better world. There were hard times before and during the war and we
   suffered. We scrimped and got along as best we could. But, once the war was
   over, we thought we were in for glory days then.

J̲OHN̲ P̲ULLEY̲

   I think for young people, 17 or 18 years of age, it was a time of tremendous
   excitement – a real contrast to these days when there's so much talk about
   political apathy and so on.

   There hadn't been a general election since about 1935 because the one that
   should have come was postponed by the war. Any meetings, we'd just jump on
   our bikes and we'd be off to take part in them. Oh yes, there was a great deal
   of excitement about then, especially amongst the young.

EILUNED REES remembers the mood of the time, even though she was too young
to remember the actual election.

E̲ILUNED̲ R̲EES̲

   I was too young to know much about political parties but I do remember the
   tremendous optimism. The whole atmosphere was as if you were on the brink of
   a new age, a paradise. Everything was going to change – it was all going to be
   all right. There'd been a period of darkness but now we were going into a sort of
   golden age. It was an atmosphere you were very conscious of as a child – you
   didn't know why, but you had this great optimism that was absolutely wonderful.

The result of the 1945 election startled many people, not least Atlee himself – not so
much the victory as its margin. The number of Labour MPs increased from 166 to
393 while conservative members decreased to just 213. In Wales, Labour took
twenty-five of the thirty-six seats, twenty of them with absolute margins. However,
for some people, like HARRY RADCLIFFE, the result was not unexpected.

HARRY RADCLIFFE

Well, it was all Labour up here, wasn't it? You might – though not very often – have had a Conservative standing but it was always Labour that got in. When they won the election in 1945, we thought we were going to be in God's Heaven, we really thought it was glory days.

JOHN PULLEY

I can't remember whether we expected Labour to win or the Tories. We usually went with the tide and that year it was a pretty strong tide. The general feeling was that things were going to be different – post-war reconstruction, that was the phrase.

There was a strong feeling that came up through the services and it percolated right through. Youngsters – and I can only speak for my friends and me – we were all rooting for a Labour victory.

HERBERT WILLIAMS was a young boy in Aberystwyth at the time and as far as he was concerned the election result was never in doubt.

HERBERT WILLIAMS

I expected Labour to win because *The Daily Mirror* said they would. It was gospel, then, *The Daily Mirror*. And I wanted them to win. So, at that age, naturally, what you want is what you tend to think is going to happen.

My brother Victor was a great Labour supporter and I tended to follow him in those matters. He used to have the *Reynolds News* on a Sunday – a very left-wing paper, long since disappeared. And, of course, *The Mirror*. It was full of the voting, votes for the troops and so on.

JOHN PULLEY was called up soon after the election and went on to serve in the Far East. He remembers the feeling and mood in those immediate post-war years.

JOHN PULLEY

I was at the Officer Training School in Bangalore and the Chief Weapons Training Officer was a pre-war regular Warrant Officer. Like a lot of them, he'd been commissioned during the war. Anyway, something cropped up and he said 'Things aren't going to be like they used to be.' And he really meant it. His Company Commander used to go hunting three days a week. That was the old army, that was how it used to be.

The war had ended, the forces of tyranny were defeated and a new government – perhaps the first true government of the people – was in office. The future beckoned brightly. There was one major problem and Atlee and his cabinet knew it – Britain was virtually bankrupt!

Chapter Two

Coming Home

THE PROCESS of demobilizing the thousands of soldiers, seamen and airmen – not to mention women in the WAAF, WRNS and ATS – who had enlisted for war service was both long and complex.

In 1945, Britain may well have been bankrupt but she still held a position of power in the world. The British Empire was on its last legs but was still in existence and armed forces were needed in places as far-flung and diverse as India, Burma, Malaysia and Palestine. While soldiers were waiting to be demobbed, they could easily find themselves engaged in policing native states in India and Burma. They might find themselves fighting anti-guerrilla campaigns in countries where the population had suddenly realised that they could gain independence by military action. Or perhaps they were trying to keep the peace in countries that had been promised freedom at the end of the war and were incensed by slow progress towards independence.

Prisoners of war were invariably given a special welcome when they finally got home – parties, speeches and often a gift of money or a cheque from the people of their home community.

Sometimes the waiting troops were involved simply in tidying up the after-effects of conflict. GLYN MILLER was engaged in exactly that type of activity in Burma.

GLYN MILLER

The Japanese surrender was, I think, in August 1945 and I was home just after Easter 1946. There was no one to fight of course but there were temporary graves to be moved into what eventually became the Military Cemeteries. I was in Signals and, obviously, we had a lot to do with that process. It all had to be recorded and messages sent back to Delhi and London. The war was winding down – well, had finished really – and we were winding down with it, I guess.

Demobilization was simply a case of waiting until your number came up.

BARBARA JONES

You all had a demob number and every now and again there'd be a list up on the board, numbers that were due for release. If your number was there, you were more or less told what to do – the process began and before you knew it you were out.

For some servicemen like ROY CHAPMAN, demobilization had come early – but only after a wide range of experiences he might otherwise never have known.

ROY CHAPMAN

I'd volunteered early in the war but it wasn't until 1943 that I was actually called on. I went to St John's Wood for initial training, then up to Leicester to do my training in flying. From there I was sent to Canada on the old *Queen Elizabeth*. We went right across the Atlantic without any escorts at all – she just relied on speed.

We landed in New York and I had the rare distinction of seeing every major liner in the world there in the dock – with the exception of the *Queen Mary* which always alternated with the *Queen Elizabeth*.

It was only later, after training, that I developed a bit of a problem. At high level, when we were using oxygen, I was beginning to get what divers called 'the bends' – nitrogen bubbles forming in the blood. Now they put this down to the fact that I have a very rare blood-group. What it meant was that I came out before the actual end of the war.

The demob process itself was not long – once it had begun. Most soldiers were through the formalities and heading towards home within a day. GLYN MILLER, JOHN PULLEY and BARBARA JONES remember what it felt like.

GLYN MILLER

I was demobbed in September 1946. When I came back from Burma, I had a fairly generous repatriation leave and then went up to Yorkshire and stayed there until I was demobbed. That was in York, Fulford Barracks, on 21st September, I think. After that I was given demob leave which expired on Boxing Day. I was on full pay and, as I remember it, with a ration allowance as well.

JOHN PULLEY

There was more than one centre, but I went up to York. You simply packed your kit and got on a train – as usual, with a rail warrant which people rather took for granted in those days.

You trekked to a great warehouse and, in the usual army way, there was a great row of desks with chaps behind them, stamping this, stamping that. You signed this, signed that and then you went off and got your clothing – from the rows and rows of suits. You had everything, even down to a hat.

This process was always the same, everyone did it. I suppose it even went on into the days of National Service, once that began.

BARBARA JONES

You had a small medical, not a full one like you had when you went in. You could keep one uniform – shirt, jacket, all your skirts and underclothes (which were your own anyway because you didn't wear the service issue). And the raincoat or the greatcoat. Most of us took the raincoat because you could wear that with civvies.

Women in the services were allowed to keep one uniform for fairly obvious reasons.

BARBARA JONES

You had to have something to go home in. Men were given a demob suit – and shoes and a trilby. You could always pick out the men who'd just been demobbed because they all had the same air-force-blue trilby.

Women? Well, they couldn't give them all the same type of suit. There were four or five to choose from for the men but with the women they gave you extra coupons and a clothing allowance once you were demobbed. You'd buy your own clothes, then you could decide what you wanted or needed.

GLYN MILLER

Demob took just one day, as I remember it. I went fairly early in the morning to Fulford Barracks. We had a medical and we were given a demob book – whether that came from your unit a few days earlier I don't remember.

Then it was just a case of choosing a demob suit, shoes and all that. If we wanted to keep the greatcoat – which I did – we were charged fifteen shillings for it.

Choosing your demob suit was a simple enough affair.

GLYN MILLER

It was rather like going into a tailor's shop because there were all sorts of sizes and different patterns. Most people, I remember, chose what came to be known as 'the demob suit' which was grey with a fine short stripe. I didn't want one of those – it was just like going out of one uniform into another. So I chose a tweed suit. It was my size and the pattern was fairly acceptable.

BARBARA JONES

So you had your uniform to go out in and you had about seven weeks' leave. And you were paid for that seven weeks, during which time you could wear your uniform, if you wanted. I think I wore mine only once after I came home.

I was lucky, I still had some of my clothes from before I'd gone away. A lot of women had been in the services for five or six years – they didn't have much at all.

For the families of men and women in the services the wait for demobilization was long and anxious, particularly if their loved one was serving in Palestine or some other area where trouble was a daily event. The waiting was hard to take. After all, the war was over. Why couldn't the soldiers just get on a ship and come home? It was a difficult question to answer.

Merthyr Tydfil Conservative Club celebrates VE Day – a much more formal affair than the impromptu street parties.

For many, the sense of separation was heightened by the presence of foreign troops on Welsh soil. Although the war in Europe had ended in May 1945, American GIs, as well as Italian and German prisoners of war, were still to be found in the country, in some instances as late as 1947 and 1948.

HERBERT WILLIAMS and ROBERT NISBET – both of whom were later to carve out careers for themselves as writers – remember the Americans and, in particular, the sentence that became a household phrase in the late 1940s: 'Got any gum, chum?'

HERBERT WILLIAMS

It was curious. I remember the arrival of soldiers in Aberystwyth – it caused great excitement amongst the local women, which was understandable.

Even Scotsmen, with incomprehensible Glaswegian accents, were regarded as something romantic because they were so different.

GIs arrived at the end of the war. I remember them coming – 'Got any gum, chum?' we'd say. Now they were really romantic figures because they were people who were in films, weren't they, Americans? Film stars!

ROBERT NISBET

One memory that sticks out in the mind, it can't have been long after the end of the war, is being told by a few of the other boys that there were Americans in town, American soldiers. And if you went up to them and said 'Got any gum, chum?' they'd give you chewing gum.

The sweet rationing was still on and the thought of free chewing gum was just too much. So I approached this very large American soldier – I can't remember what rank he was but he seemed to be a very big man. This was on St Thomas' Green in Haverfordwest. I walked up to him, went through the mantra – 'Got any gum, chum?' – and sure enough he produced what, looking back, I think was a ten pack of Wrigleys.

Now, the five pack of Wrigleys was the norm so this ten pack was absolute luxury. I was probably never quite so grateful to any man as I was to that one American soldier. I chewed them for weeks and weeks – I eked them out, as you would in those days, until every last shred of sugar had left the things.

Welsh writer Robert Nisbet in a photograph taken just after the end of hostilities.

HERBERT WILLIAMS

> Next door to our playground wall was an open space where a lot of American
> GIs were billeted. And I remember some of the boys in our school blowing up
> these curious objects which, in my innocence, looked like balloons! Of course,
> they weren't balloons. You can imagine what they were.
>
> So, in a way, the Americans introduced a lot of sex education – in a very
> primitive way.

For MARCO CARINI, living in his father's café and shop at Beaufort, it was the
Italian prisoners of war who made their presence felt.

MARCO CARINI

> Every Sunday my father would have a visit from two prisoners from the
> Crickhowell Camp, Italian prisoners of war. There were more than just Italians
> there in the camp, there were Germans as well, but it was the Italians who
> came up to us.
>
> They used to bring fresh eggs and fresh tomatoes up to my father every
> Sunday. Then they'd spend the day there, in the shop.

It was the sense of being lost and lonely, marooned far away from home, that made
people stop and think – their own loved ones were in the same position, thousands
of miles away from Wales. So, in general, the foreign soldiers on Welsh soil, like
Marco Carini's Italians, were treated with kindness and respect.

As the months dragged on, more and more soldiers were demobbed and soon the
trickle became a stream. And then the happiness of everyone, from the demobbed
soldier to his ecstatic family, was unsurpassed.

HERBERT WILLIAMS

> Oh, it was a joy when my brother Richard came home. I did miss him very
> much as he was the next brother up from me. And I'd followed his progress in
> the RAF very closely.
>
> The sad thing, on my part, was that he wasn't home for very long before he
> went off again – to study Physics at Birmingham University.

ROBERT NISBET

> The boy next door, the older brother of my two friends, he came back from
> Archangel. He'd been active on the convoys and the story of his return was
> famous in the Lane's history – I say the Lane because that's where we all lived.
>
> I think the look of toned-down rapture on the face of his mother as this boy,
> who'd been away at the age of twenty, to Archangel and back, walked safely
> up the drive, was amazing.

Sometimes, if a soldier or airman had been a prisoner of war he might need medical
assistance – or even just fattening up – before he was finally judged fit enough to be
demobbed. EILUNED REES remembers her brother's return from a German POW

camp, some time after the war had ended. Flying in the RAF, he had been shot down over Germany in the last year of the war and for several weeks his family had not known his fate. His release, however, did not come immediately.

EILUNED REES

I can't remember the exact date he came back but I do remember going to meet him. He arrived at Carmarthen station and we'd gone to meet him in Dai Carrier's taxi – Dai Carrier was David Thomas who ran a carrier business and a big garage in the village

I think my father must have been with us – and the Baptist Minister's son, who had come for the ride. And my brother looked so very, very thin, after being a prisoner at the end of the war. Time had elapsed before they'd sent him home. They'd fed him up a bit but he still looked very, very thin.

We're not a demonstrative family – to put it mildly – and my opening gambit was not to throw my arms around him and tell him how glad I was to see him but to announce to him that he'd won a medal. To which he replied 'What for?' and I said 'I don't know but you've got one.' It was the DFC. He never told us why he'd got it but, obviously, it was for some act of bravery.

The return of soldiers or airmen, sailors or Royal Marines, was often met by huge banners strung across the street or the front of the house, as MYRTLE JENKINS and BARBARA JONES recall.

MYRTLE JENKINS

When my husband Dai came back we celebrated as best we could. They had flags right from one end of the street to the bottom. And signs that said 'Welcome Home Dai.' It gave you a wonderful feeling. I'd lived there in that street for twenty-five years so they all knew me so well.

BARBARA JONES

Often, if somebody was being demobbed, you'd see flags out and a big banner – 'Welcome Home Jimmy' or whoever. I can remember a cartoon which I thought was funny. As I say, it was a common thing to see the banners up – 'Welcome Home So and So, Two Years in Burma' or 'Three Years in

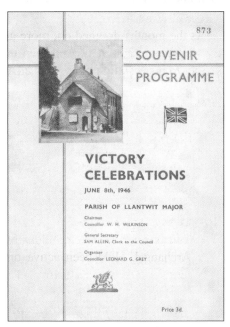

Official Victory Celebrations often took place many months after the end of the war. This Souvenir Programme from Llantwit Major marks the event twelve months after peace was declared.

Italy.' Or something. And this cartoon, it was 'Welcome Home Mum, Five Hours in the Fish Queue.' I've always remembered that.

For most people who were leaving the forces, the strongest emotion was relief. Many of them had enjoyed the experience but that could not hide their pleasure and joy at being free from military discipline at least.

GLYN MILLER

I was glad to be out of the army, just like I'd been glad to get in when it all started. I'd volunteered as soon as I was 18 and while it took some time to finally get in, I was just as keen to get out when the war was over.

For some, returning home brought strange experiences – like that of CHARLIE STERRY when he returned to Wales in August 1945.

CHARLIE STERRY

I caught my train to Newport and when I got off there wasn't a soul on the platform, except for one person right down on the other end waiting to catch a train. It was my sister and she was waiting to catch the train back to Marshfield. I'd left home in 1939 and this was 1945 – and the first person I met was my own sister.

Sometimes returning soldiers brought all sorts of emotions in their wake – everything from anger to tears. At this distance it is often difficult to even begin to catch the sheer joy that accompanied the reunion of people who had not seen each other for many months – or, for that matter, the wonder of returning to a place that had been dreamed about for years. DAVID and MYRTLE JENKINS recall how they felt.

DAVID JENKINS

We got to Abercynon and then we were able to see Aberdare. All the pimples were rising out of my skin.

My father and brother, they'd met every train that day, every train on the Low Level station. And they waited until the very last one. 'Oh, he won't be on this one,' they said. But I was, I was there on the Milk Train as they called it.

I gave them a big hug – I was very close to my brother, very close. Then it was over to Myrtle's house. And she knew it was me because on my haversack I had a small mug and it hit against the wall – 'Oh, it's Dai.' A big hug and a kiss, then. We just couldn't say anything. But, oh, it was lovely to be back in Aberdare, lovely it was.

MYRTLE JENKINS

It was so strange, the first night he came back. I found it strange to put my arm under his. My mother and I always walked, you know, and I always had her arm, my arm on top. When Dai came home, I felt really strange with a man there on my arm.

It was a time of high emotion and sometimes people got things wrong. For some, the sense of tragedy lingered, long after the moment, as JACK CARRADICE and EILUNED REES testify.

JACK CARRADICE

I remember when I came back from India, I upset my mother by going, first of all, to Pembroke Dock to see Mary. My mother thought I should have gone home to Barnard Castle first. At the time it never entered my head – I wanted to see the girl I was going to marry. Up till then we'd only talked about marriage in letters. Later on I began to see quite how much I'd upset my mother – well, I'd been away for nearly five years. I suppose she had a point.

EILUNED REES

Dai Carrier, in the village, had one son who contracted some obscure disease out in the Far East. He was sent home. But, because troops were released over a period of years, he didn't come back until 1947, in the middle of the big snow.

He got as far as Carmarthen. Now Llansteffan was isolated for quite a while that year, being eight miles from Carmarthen and snowed up. But, the people of the village, they thought it was urgent to get to Carmarthen to fetch Dolph – that was Dai's son.

And so all the men got into Dai Carrier's lorry and dug their way into town. I don't remember how long it took them but I can remember the tension at our end. After all, we didn't know whether they'd made it, whether something had happened, whether somebody had fallen off or the lorry had got stuck. It was quite an anxious time in the village as dusk was approaching.

It was a case of everybody out. We were all on the streets waiting. And I can still remember, vividly, a shout going up – 'They're coming!' And then we heard the rumble of the lorry and as they came up the hill we were all cheering.

And I was terribly proud because there was my father, all six foot of him, in his policeman's cloak and his policeman's hat, brandishing his spade. And they brought Dai Carrier's son back.

Sadly, he died soon afterwards. It was tragic. Dolph was so young, a nice boy. There was a great deal of unhappiness in the village when he went.

For those who had lost loved ones in the war, the coming of peace and the returning of soldiers was a bitter-sweet affair. LINDA WESTERMAN had lost her husband and two brothers, all within eleven months of each other.

LINDA WESTERMAN

We got married in January 1943 and my husband was called up in May. He was killed in August 1944. He was in the air force, a mid-upper gunner. But previous to that I'd also lost two brothers. My one brother got killed at sea and my eldest brother was in the army and he was killed at Salerno. And then, of course, my husband. All within eleven months of each other.

I was devastated, to tell the truth. Thank God I had my mother and father – they pulled me through it. My father said 'You'll never want.'

But then, life has to go on. You can't sit and grieve for ever. I never forget but you have to move on. You've got to think about your children – and I was pregnant when my husband was killed. My daughter was born six weeks later.

RON SUMPTION was just sixteen when the war ended and his memories of the end of hostilities are also tinged with sadness.

RON SUMPTION

I can remember, vividly, VE Day and VJ Day, when the war officially ended. It means a lot – because my father had been killed. He'd been a prisoner of war in Japan and the family was upset because they knew other people would be coming back. And he wouldn't.

His father had died when the ship on which he was travelling, a Japanese prisoner-of-war vessel, was torpedoed by an American submarine. It was an ironic, tragic way to die.

RON SUMPTION

I can't really remember my feelings now. I was obviously upset, knowing that I wouldn't see my father again but I don't think it was made any worse when I saw the other soldiers come home. I think that, as a family, we were just grateful that the war was over and that there'd be no more people killed.

Ron Sumption's father had been a RSM in a Territorial Unit from the Rhondda. Along with the rest of his battalion, he was captured in Java in 1943. Very few of them ever made it back to the Rhondda.

RON SUMPTION

Most of the people in that unit died. Very few of them, the Territorials that my father had been with, ever made it back. The ones that did were in a hell of a mess, physically. And my mother used to say 'I'm glad your father didn't come back if he was going to be like that.'

Coming to terms with her husband's death did not come easily for Ron Sumption's mother but it was something she knew she had to do.

RON SUMPTION

My mother was a very resilient woman but it took her a while. Initially I think she had a few spasms of depression but, by and large, it went after a while. She came to terms with it, I think.

There may have been a little flash of bitterness at one stage, at the end of the war, but it didn't last long. Generally speaking she – all of us – were so pleased the war was over.

The death of a loved one was never easy to accept and, at the end of the war, reality hit home for many people. The support of family was particularly necessary.

LINDA WESTERMAN

If it hadn't been for my mother and father, where would I have been? I'd have been in the drink. I couldn't have afforded to go into rooms or pay rent so they more or less kept me going. The war widows' pension then was nothing – I think I was having about £5 to keep me and the baby.

Linda Westerman's husband had worked with her in the armaments factory at Glascoed before he had joined the RAF. She had several options open to her, ways of increasing her meagre pension, but her parents were adamant about what she should do.

LINDA WESTERMAN

I said 'I can get help from the naval armaments people' but my father was clear. He said 'You don't want charity. Don't you dare apply.'

The forces, the army, navy and air force, they also look after their war widows, don't they. If you find your pension is not enough you can apply. My father wouldn't hear of it – nor my mother.

'You dad's working,' she said. 'You live. You keep your little bit of pension. We'll all manage.'

I felt so guilty but my father was clear – 'That's what families are for,' he said. 'If I can't look after my own then it's time I wrapped it all up.'

So they worked to keep me, I suppose. Otherwise I wouldn't have had a roof over my head. I'll never forget them.

For SYLVIA BAILEY, loss, when it came, was totally unexpected. Her father was in a reserved occupation and not in the armed forces at all. He worked for the Electricity Board at a power station in Colchester Avenue in Cardiff and was killed when the plant was bombed – on a day when he was not due to be working at all. He had simply called in to work to pick up his wages.

SYLVIA BAILEY

When I say his death didn't really register, it shows how differently children react to death. He was just dead. I remember going to school and almost saying 'My father was killed last week.' That's how you are when you're seven. You think they're going to come back, you don't think this is final. Not until later – it was years later, after the war ended – that I realised the significance of it.

Sylvia Bailey's father, Arthur Richard Bryant, had been killed when a bomb was dropped on the SWEB power station in 1942. This photograph shows him at work in the power station.

For most people in Wales, however, the return of loved ones meant simply an opportunity to celebrate. In many instances returning soldiers were given a hero's welcome, no matter what they had done during the war. If someone had served his or her country in any capacity then that was reason enough to throw a party.

In cases like the Crescent in Merthyr Vale, where 130 men from the street served in the armed forces during the war, such celebration was certainly well deserved – it has to be a record for the number of men serving in the armed forces from just one street. Many of the returning servicemen in towns like Merthyr Tydfil were given gifts of money, collected from the people of the town – it was a way of saying 'Welcome home, welcome back.'

HUBERT 'BUZZER' REYNOLDS

There were street parties in lots of places. People just put all their bits and pieces together. They really did very, very well.

EILUNED REES

The homecomings were tremendous. They had a welcome home party for everybody – a dozen at least. I still don't know where they got all the food from but there was a meal for everyone. I think people used to save up their coupons and then pool their rations. There were always cakes and sponges. They really put on a good spread.

And then there'd be a 'Do it Yourself' concert as well. I can remember performing in them. One, in particular, I remember. You had to talk for a minute on a given subject – Pinocchio and the Barber won but I came second. Not bad for a little girl.

For most of the returning soldiers or sailors or airmen the one thing they wanted – and needed – was a little peace and quiet. Holiday was the first concern for many after years spent digging fox-holes or sitting in some God-forsaken jungle hell-hole. Work could come later, after a little relaxation – as GLYN MILLER remembers.

GLYN MILLER

After I was demobbed I came back to Bridgend. I didn't look for work straightaway, I was just enjoying my leave. I met one or two friends I hadn't seen since the early days of the war. We went dancing in the Palais de Dance in Bridgend or in the Grand Pavilion in Porthcawl. We also went to the pictures a great deal, I seem to remember. And girls, of course, we were dating girls.

I also remember going down to see Swansea Town play. They were, in the Second Division then, I think. We watched them play every Saturday – well, every other Saturday, I suppose. Then it was the pictures in Swansea and home by the late train because we didn't have cars in those days.

What else did we do? Very little. Pubs, of course, we used to inhabit the pubs a great deal. I suppose it was because our days were our own, we didn't have work to do. It was a real luxury having nothing to do. But we were always thinking that work had to come along some time.

BARBARA JONES

I came straight back to Cardiff once I was demobbed. I think I was home for about a month and by then I was getting a bit fed up because most of my friends were working. So I just thought it was time to look for a job.

For the vast majority of people who had served on the Home Front – men and women in reserved occupations, engaged in work of national importance – the luxury of a month or two without work did not come into the equation. HUBERT 'BUZZER' REYNOLDS was a fireman and his job did not end with the cessation of hostilities.

Hubert 'Buzzer' Reynolds, resplendent in his fireman's uniform.

HUBERT 'BUZZER' REYNOLDS

> The work carried on after the war. The danger was still there, all night long, but it was not as immediate as it was during the war. Then you just didn't know where it was coming from. After the war we came off twelve-hour duties onto eight-hour ones. You didn't have the same tension that you had during the war.

MARCO CARINI was a young boy in 1945, living with his family over their shop in Beaufort. His father had been interned, along with thousands of other Italian immigrants, but at the end of hostilities the business had to continue – and it was not easy.

MARCO CARINI

> I think it got a bit harder for the family and the shop after the war. My father was running the café side of things. He'd stopped going out with the ice cream because the carts had gone through the war and deteriorated. The horse had gone – they'd lost him on the mountain. So he just stuck to the shop.
>
> He opened another one in Brynmawr, for fish and chips. And he did the two shops. He'd go to Brynmawr until half past four, then he'd come back and run the Beaufort shop.
>
> A lot of difficult people came in to the shops, really nasty people who'd lost children in the war or perhaps relatives in London. And they blamed the Italians. So we had a lot of abuse – 'Get back to Italy,' they'd say. Things like that.

In the main, however, the mood in Wales at that time was one of hope and expectation. The soldiers knew that their years in the services were over. Now it was time to pick up the pieces and start again.

Marco Carini's mother, shown here serving in the family shop and café in Beaufort after the end of the war.

Chapter Three

Not Just the Soldiers

READJUSTMENT to life outside the services was something that everyone had to face in the years after 1945, not just the soldiers. It involved everyone in the family – wives, and children, fathers and mothers, friends and relatives alike.

And for many people that readjustment was not easy. For couples who had married before or during the war, there might well have been years of enforced separation. If a man was serving in the Far East then the chance of leave – or, at least, a long enough leave to enable him to travel home – was remote. In some instances soldiers were away for five or six years at a stretch.

MYRTLE and DAVID JENKINS were married in 1942 but less than a fortnight later he was posted abroad. It was the beginning of a long absence.

MYRTLE JENKINS

We were only married twelve days before he went off. He was away for three and a half years. Then he came home, supposedly for a month but actually he was granted another month as his mother had had a heart attack. And then he went back again and I didn't see him for another couple of years. It was five years altogether that we were separated.

For many women, release from the forces – as well as the demob of their loved ones – meant marriage, children and settling down.

The effect of an absence like that was different with different people. They reacted to it according to their personality. Many events that, normally, would be taken for granted had to be put on hold. It was only when soldiers returned for good from the war that their significance became apparent.

MYRTLE JENKINS

Our first wedding anniversary together was actually our sixth. Imagine that!

DAVID JENKINS

> I was in Italy when the war ended and they sent us home from there. I sent Myrtle an airgraph. It was like a small letter because we couldn't send proper ones. It said 'Arrive today, home tomorrow.' Oh, it was wonderful.
>
> We got on the plane and sat there until we landed in Peterborough Transit Camp. The RAF bloke said, 'You all right, Taff? Had a good trip?' 'Oh it was great,' I said. 'We're home.' He smiled. 'You're lucky,' he said. 'You're sitting on the bomb doors.'
>
> It was a wonderful feeling, mind. Some of the boys were living around the London area and they were allowed home straight away. We weren't. We were told we'd got to stay until we could go home the following day.
>
> And we did. We went home the next day.

MYRTLE JENKINS

> It was a wonderful thing, being together again. Nobody'll ever take it away. Nor that moment we met again after all those years.
>
> He came through the door and he said 'Myrt' and I said 'Dai.' That's all we could say. Then we just caught around each other. After all that time, it was a bit strange at first but it was a wonderful feeling. I get choked up thinking about it even now.

Myrtle and David Jenkins were lucky. Their relationship was strong enough to survive the separation. Others weren't as fortunate. Part of the trouble came from the very nature of the human personality. All too often people grew and changed during the time they were apart. In some cases – as with Myrtle and David Jenkins – love became stronger, in others it broke into fragments. Even if partners were totally committed to each other, when the man finally came home, a successful relationship meant having to adjust attitudes and behaviours on both sides.

Men in the services had been used to taking and giving orders. They had been used to attacking problems, not skirting around the edges. Debate and discussion were not always useful: there was a normal way of doing things and an army way. And many servicemen found the civilian way of getting on not exactly to their liking.

Being in civvy street once again, where rank and medals meant absolutely nothing and where there were no comrades to support them, many felt totally lost. Some marriages and many relationships with children foundered.

If the returning soldier had endured a particularly torrid time, then his homecoming was never going to be easy. There was no counselling or help for trauma victims in those days – as ESTELLE CLARKE remembers.

ESTELLE CLARKE

> I had a friend whose husband had been a prisoner of war in Japan. When he came home he weighed just six and a half stone. He was a walking skeleton. He was unbearable to live with because his nerves were just shattered.
>
> They had a young child – she was just four then and he couldn't stand the

noise. Can you imagine the battle, trying to keep a child of that age quiet because her father's nerves were in such a state? It was dreadful.

Even for well-grounded relationships, the war had inflicted such horrific experiences on soldiers that it was bound to impinge on the way they felt and behaved.

ESTELLE CLARKE

We'd grown up, Bob and me, such a lot and it took a lot of readjustment, a great deal of readjustment, because we'd both matured to such an extent. He'd seen such horrors. And I suppose I had too, in a different sort of way.

Sometimes problems were not just emotional, particularly for soldiers who had served in the Far East.

MARY PHILLIPS

Jack used to have regular bouts – well, I don't know if it was malaria or not, but if it wasn't then it was pretty bad flu. We just had to put him to bed and keep him there. It went on for several years.

ESTELLE CLARKE

I think we were some of the lucky ones because Bob came back. The only thing he suffered from was malaria. He had one bad attack of that. Fortunately, my father knew what it was and said 'Quick, all the hot water bottles you can find. And all the eiderdowns, pile them on the top.' And that cured the malaria.

For a country that had just been through one of the most dramatic conflicts of the century, there were still a great many 'puritan' attitudes around. JOAN SMITH, MAISIE WILLIAMS, BARBARA JONES and SYLVIA BAILEY all recall how some people felt about divorce and broken marriages – and about how things began to change after the war.

JOAN SMITH

When a man came back from the war it was often different – sometimes their wives had found other men. Having said that, it was still frowned upon, divorce, failed marriages and that.

I remember, when I was about sixteen, this woman being pointed out to me in a shop. She was a divorced woman! It was, you know, shocking. And I thought – well I didn't know the standards or anything – I was amazed to see she was so pretty and attractive. And yet she was divorced!

It's funny, now, but you were always told that they were common sorts, for want of a better phrase, to get into a position like that, for a marriage to break up. Standards have totally changed now, of course, but that's how people felt then. They just didn't know any better.

MAISIE WILLIAMS

I think it was the women working in places like the armaments factories that changed things. A lot of us were narrow-minded when we went in but in the factory there was more open talk – you learned about different things from one another.

BARBARA JONES

There was a WAAF girl working with me in Sherman's after the war and a lot of the girls would find out that we'd been in the forces. They'd say that they'd have loved to have gone but their mothers wouldn't let them. Of course we'd say 'Why not?' 'Oh no,' they'd say, 'they didn't know what we'd get up to.'

We got this saying off pat – 'Oh yes? She judged others by herself, did she?' That usually didn't go down well.

Or maybe you'd hear women say 'Oh I wouldn't let my daughter go.' We'd respond by saying 'Oh, you judged others by your own standards, did you?'

SYLVIA BAILEY

An aunt and uncle of mine – he'd been in the navy – they had four children and this aunt was 40 by this time. Well, he came back from the war and to everyone's astonishment she was found to be having a baby. It's nothing now, having a baby at that age, but then it was a case of 'Oh dear me, she's having another baby!' It was frowned on, shocking!

There were never any guarantees about relationships picking up after years of disharmony and discord but if people were prepared to work at things, there was every hope of success. And in many cases it was better not to have too many preconceptions, as MARY PHILLIPS and BARBARA JONES have stated.

MARY PHILLIPS

Jack and I had only spent a few months together – and then only as a boyfriend/girlfriend. When he went away to India I had no idea we were going to end up together. That sort of developed as we wrote to each other over the years.

He was away for four years and when he came back – after

Home from the WAAF, Mary Phillips waits for her demob – still wearing her uniform, you will note.

all the emotion of seeing him, of course – it was a case of starting to learn all about each other. We had no history, nothing to base it on. We were starting from the beginning. And I think that was the best way, really.

BARBARA JONES

I knew my husband before I joined the WRNS. We were going out together but I got fed up and we split. I was demobbed just before him – he'd been out in Burma. We got back together after that and married in 1949. I don't know how it would have worked if we'd stayed together.

For many ex-service people it was the comradeship they missed most.

BARBARA JONES

You missed the company. It was a good life, the WRNS. I did enjoy it. We had a good crowd of girls. You always had your own special friend but always company as well. Somebody'd be going ashore and say 'Anybody coming?' If you didn't want to do anything else you'd go. There was always something to do, plenty of amusement.

When I first came out I don't think I noticed it much. It was afterwards, when I went to work, that I felt it. Then I missed the people – and the way of life. And another thing, in the morning, in the forces, you got up and knew exactly what you'd be wearing. Of course, when you came home you had to think 'Have I got this? Have I washed that?' You didn't have that many clothes to choose from – so that was something very different.

For GLYN MILLER and ROY CHAPMAN, like many ex-servicemen, it was only when they had been demobbed that they realised that the closeness of army and air-force life had gone forever. They tried to create substitute support mechanisms of their own but it was not easy.

GLYN MILLER

For the first year, of course, we had a large number of ex-servicemen working with us in the Income Tax Office in Bridgend. We used to go out at lunchtime and have a pint with our lunch. And we'd meet several times a week, so we kept up a certain amount of comradeship. We would also meet in the evenings – not all that often because, of course, several of us were married by then – but, yes, we kept up a degree of comradeship, I suppose.

ROY CHAPMAN

For the first couple of months it was very strange. It was just the totally different environment. I missed the comradeship to start with, the comradeship that we had in the RAF at that time. When I came back quite a few of my pals were still away in the forces, my previous friends that is. We all joined up later so it didn't last too long and I settled into the old routine. But it was strange to start with.

For DAVID JENKINS, who spent most of the war in the Middle East and Italy, it was wonderful coming back home to Aberdare but settling down was still hard.

DAVID JENKINS

> Oh it was difficult, very, very difficult. I've said that many times to Myrtle, my wife – Duw, I said, I do miss my mates. And we did genuinely miss each other. There was such a lot of comradeship in the army.

His feelings did not last long, however. As with most returning soldiers, it was an emotion that came and went fairly quickly.

DAVID JENKINS

> I didn't feel it at first, it came after a month or two, once I'd got organised with a job. Different people had begun to come back, friends like Ron Edmonds – he was a fitter with the Red and White. He'd been in the RAF. Different people were coming back and then we'd get talking to each other – 'Do you miss it?' 'Oh, aye, I miss the comradeship.'
>
> It came after a while, you know? And then, gradually it went. Like when I first went abroad. I was homesick but, gradually, that disappeared. And it was the same thing with the comradeship. After a while – I'd say about twelve months – it went. We had children coming along by then and I think that helped. Yes, it probably helped a lot.

Adjusting to work in civilian life was not always easy as many men came out of the forces with pre-set attitudes and preconceptions. Many of them had been conditioned by their experiences and by their training. JACK CARRADICE and ESTELLE CLARKE experienced exactly that situation.

JACK CARRADICE

> I think I had a few problems adjusting to civilian life – like lots of returning soldiers, I suppose. I got a job in the old dockyard at Pembroke Dock – before the war I'd just finished my apprenticeship as an electrician up on Tyneside. And when I went to the dockyard I thought 'Well there is this job to do, let's get on and do it.' That was how it had been before the war on Tyneside and in the army as well.
>
> But in the dockyard the lads, well, they didn't want any of that. 'Slow down,' they'd say. 'If we finish this job they'll only give us another. Sit down here and have a fag.' I couldn't cope with that, it was alien to me. And that certainly caused me a few problems.

ESTELLE CLARKE

> Bob, my husband, he'd been training with a firm as a draughtsman and after the war he returned to the same firm. There were six of them, in all, coming back. And they got very annoyed with some of the workmen who'd obviously

skived a lot during the war. They started telling some very gory stories at lunchtime and they weren't very popular.

In the end he was so fed up with it that he gave it up and went back into the army. He became a regular serviceman.

It wasn't just ex-servicemen who felt the loss of companionship, as Land Army Girls DORIS CURTIS and JOAN MACDONALD can testify. And keeping in touch with friends made during the years of crisis and trouble was important.

DORIS CURTIS

It did take you a while to adjust. When you'd been with a crowd of girls like that you missed the companionship. Because we were a good crowd together, about twenty-four or twenty-six of us in all.

I kept up some friendships after I'd left the Land Army. One friend lived near Manchester and when I went up home, on holiday, I'd always go and see her. I kept friends with her for many years, until she died. The others, you just drifted away from, I suppose.

JOAN MACDONALD

In 1989 I found one of the Land Army Girls I had been with on the farm. She'd moved to Ross-on-Wye. So then I decided to try and find the others who'd worked on the same farm for four years between 1942 and 1946. I managed to contact five of them and we had a reunion after 55 years. We've met every year since then. What a joy it is! It always seems as if we had never been parted.

In 2001 Joan MacDonald organised a reunion of the Land Army Girls she had served with during the war. This shows her (front left) along with fellow Land Army girls Sylvia, Doris, Dora and Glenys. In the background is a photograph of the same women in 1942.

Children often found it difficult to accept their fathers when they suddenly appeared in the house again – in some cases after being away for many years. BARBARA JONES remembers the time and feelings.

BARBARA JONES

I had a step-uncle and his little boy was a few months old when he went off to the war. He was in North Africa and, I think, Italy. Then he was out in Burma until the war over there was ended. And he hadn't had leave in all that time.

This little boy was in school when the man came back. So his father – well, he was a stranger, wasn't he? He'd had a picture of his father but that picture was nothing like the man who eventually came home.

And the man, of course, he had to get used to this strange child – just like the child had to get used to the strange man.

They didn't like it, the children. They'd had their mothers all to themselves up until then. I knew several couples that applied to. One man was very upset – he never did get on with his daughter, never did. She just wouldn't take to him at all. It never got any better – they just tolerated each other. It was awful, very sad, because he couldn't wait to get home and see this little two-year-old he had left. But, of course, when he came home she was about six. It was so sad.

MALCOLM PILE has written about the memories of his father's return from war in his book *A Cardiff Family in the Forties*. For him, as with many young children, the return of someone who had previously been referred to only in photograph and letter, led to rather mixed feelings.

MALCOLM PILE

While I liked the idea in principle, I had no concept of what it was like to share a home with a father as well as a mother. Father was only known as the sender of letters which appeared from time to time.

The actual day of his father's return was something of an anti-climax.

MALCOLM PILE

After what seemed the briefest of greetings, I was requested to go into the living room and read a book. I duly sat in the Morriston Shelter. Mother and father went upstairs to greet each other, I have no doubt, in a less inhibited manner. That was a perfectly natural and proper thing to do. As I sat in the shelter, trying to read, it did not seem quite right to me. Time went by very slowly and in any case I wanted my tea. I began to doubt whether fathers were such a good idea.

Evacuees had been sent to Wales as early as the autumn of 1939. Whilst many of them soon returned to London or Liverpool or whichever industrial centre they had come from, many more stayed on in Wales until the end of the war. And they, too, sometimes found it difficult to readjust when they went back home to live.

NORMA WAGNER and VIOLET CROPPER were both evacuated from Liverpool to the Aberystwyth area.

NORMA WAGNER

I was sent to Trefenter, up in the mountains outside Aberystwyth. I wasn't even five at the time and I was there until about 1945-46.

After the war, evacuees were supposed to go back home the same way they'd come – by train and bus. Mind you, by 1945-46 a lot had already gone and there were only a few of us left. Anyway, my mum got a letter saying that I'd be put on a train and that she should be there to meet me at the other end.

My mum was about to have a baby at the time and she wrote and asked if they could keep me a little longer. Well, payment for taking an evacuee had stopped but I stayed on for another six months, maybe even a bit longer.

VIOLET CROPPER

I was in Aberystwyth for three years. I was anxious to get home to mum. Well, she had a new baby, a new brother for us, and there was a lot of fuss about it. My first foster mum had been very nice – she even wanted to adopt me. But she died, my Aunty Annie, and I had to move. The second family was not as nice so I was quite happy to go home.

NORMA WAGNER

I found it very distressing, going back to Liverpool. I couldn't settle. I'd got used to living on a farm, a smallholding. I'd been spoiled by my grandparents – as I called them – and by their unmarried daughter. And by this time my mum had six children. So when I came home I had to do things for others, rather than have them done for me. I didn't like the hurly-burly of Liverpool.

VIOLET CROPPER

I did miss Wales, once I'd come home. I kept in contact with the Roberts family, my first foster parents – and I still do. But I didn't want to go back to Wales, mainly because my Auntie Annie Roberts had died.

Liverpool was strange, mind. It had been badly bombed since I'd been away and there was a terrible mess. My new school was big and different. I'd learned to sing in Welsh when I was in Aberystwyth in the small school and the chapel I used to go to by Trinity Place. It was nice but I didn't want to go back there to live.

NORMA WAGNER

It was traumatic, trying to fit into Liverpool. Previously I'd gone to a village school but in Liverpool my school was massive and everyone already had their own friends. It was difficult trying to fit back in.

I suppose I struggled academically – the school in Trefenter hadn't been very good and the head was only an old woodwork master from London. You were taught by the older girls: they were approaching fourteen and weren't going to the town school.

I left school in Liverpool when I was fifteen and got a job in the British American Tobacco Company. I'd been back to Wales when I was thirteen, to help bury my grandfather. I say MY grandfather because he was, in a way, part of my family. I always called them *Mamgu* and *Tadcu*.

Grandmother, that's my foster grandmother, didn't want to stay on the farm on her own and so my mum let me stay with her. I think I was there for ten months in all.

That had been only a brief stay but the lure of Wales eventually proved too strong for Norma Wagner.

NORMA WAGNER

I finally moved back to Wales for good when I was seventeen. I don't think my mother ever really forgave me. She was quite bitter for many years and there was little communication between us. I went back to Liverpool with my husband, for a visit, and called to see her – that was the first time we'd really had contact.

Returning to Wales to live was well, it was wonderful. I came back to the same part of Wales where I'd lived during the war. I'd fallen in love with the place, simple as that.

Staying on was not just a prerogative of evacuees. Many visitors and temporary residents, just like Norma Wagner, had fallen in love with Wales during their time in the country. And German prisoners of war were no exception. KONRAD MEIER, WYN TREPTE and MAX TSCHACKERT were three who decided to remain here once they were released.

MAX TSCHACKERT

I married a Welsh woman, the postman's daughter. I'd met her in the village – we were allowed out of the camp to do work on the farms each day. I worked on the farms for a long time – well, where else could I go? We were restricted. They only lifted those restrictions in 1951. I suppose, by then, attitudes had changed.

WYN TREPTE

I told myself that since I had nobody in Germany except my brother, I may as well make my home over here. And I was really determined to learn English. What I did was, I had a book in the POW camp which gave lessons in learning English.

But that wasn't enough for me. I wanted to do it quicker. So at night I used to write down 20 words and take them, the following day, to work. On the farm you didn't use much of your head, you just used brawn, so I learned those words. And when I came back at night I could read them, speak them and spell them. I made progress at a fantastic speed. In one week I had 140 new words – and this went on every week.

KONRAD MEIER

I was in the Island Farm camp at Bridgend for three years. And for some of that time I was batman for Field Marshal Von Rundstedt. We had lessons in lots of things at the camp. We organised them amongst ourselves, it wasn't done by the guards. Most of the lessons were taken by the generals. I learned English and History while I was in that camp.

MAX TSCHACKERT

I became a church warden and I was treasurer in the church. I was secretary in the Gardening Association. What happened with me was I joined everything I could.

In the beginning you had a few things thrown at you – 'Bloody German' and things. But when you told them off, when you challenged them, they usually went yellow.

WYN TREPTE

I came to Machynlleth and, over a pint in the Wynnstay, I was talking to this fellow from the Royal Welch Fusiliers. I told him I'd been taken prisoner by the Fusiliers. He said 'Good God, we took twelve or fifteen prisoners from one company in a corn field outside Caen. Halfway back there was a burned-out Sherman tank and the commander was standing there. When he saw us he pulled out his pistol as if to shoot the prisoners. Only we wouldn't let him.'

I said 'Well I was one of those prisoners. That's exactly what happened to me on the way back.' There was no bad feeling, we were just enjoying a pint, talking over our experiences.

Wyn Trepte shortly after he had settled down in Wales.

My attitude is that it was something that happened. You were involved in it because you were German, just like the others were English or Welsh. None of us could help it.

KONRAD MEIER

> After the war was over we were allowed a fair bit of freedom. A friend and I used to take a daily walk and, eventually, we arrived at the clubhouse of Southerndown Golf Club. We struck up a conversation with a lady who was working in the clubhouse and ended up sat on stools, outside the kitchen, peeling potatoes. Our reward? Five Woodbines apiece.

Konrad Meier stayed on in the Bridgend area and later became a member of Southerndown Golf Club.

KONRAD MEIER

> After I was released in 1948 – imagine that, three years as a prisoner after the war had ended – I got a job in a factory in Bridgend. I had a flat and from the bedroom window I could actually see the huts of Island Farm POW camp. It was a strange feeling.

For the Italian community in Wales, the process of internment had been a bitter blow. Thousands of hard-working Italians – many of whom had been running cafés and ice cream parlours for years in the Welsh valleys – had been rounded up and sent off to internment camps after Mussolini declared war in 1940. The majority were released, following Italy's surrender in 1943 but for some, just like the German POWs who were still behind bars two or three years after the war ended, it was not a guaranteed process. PETER SIDOLI and MARCO CARINI had different experiences of the internment procedure.

PETER SIDOLI

> My brothers were interned and although Italy was out of the war from 1943 on, they weren't released for another two years. They were sent to the Isle of Man and interned out there. They were treated well but it was a long time to be away.
>
> I visited them twice and they were okay – no complaints.

MARCO CARINI

> Most of the Italian internees came home after Italy surrendered. Some of them were home before that. My father was taken away in 1941 but he was only away just over twelve months. I don't know if the government realised its mistake and realised that they'd done no harm. Most of them, like my father, had been here in Wales for years.

PETER SIDOLI

> In general the Welsh people were very good. You'd have one or two insults but nothing much. On VE and VJ Days my father was out on the cart, selling ice cream. He was booked into every street. He started in the morning at ten and didn't finish until midnight. He had no problem.

MARCO CARINI

There was a lot of good feeling. People, everybody, talked about the internments. 'Jake (my father) shouldn't have gone', they said, 'he's a nice chap.'

I can't remember what it was like after my father came back. I should imagine it was a bit difficult for us to adjust. But remember, I had three older brothers and they carried us through.

PETER SIDOLI

You've got to remember, lots of Italian people who came to Britain to live didn't even know where a place like Sorrento was. After the war was over more British people had seen the place than any of the Italians who were living here. I was about eight years old when I came to Wales – I only heard about Salerno because of the landings there during the war.

When the soldiers started coming back, once they began to get demobbed, well they knew a lot more about Italy than I did. More about Italy than my father, even. Let's be honest, I only heard about Verdi and composers like that from the Welsh choirs!

The Second World War undoubtedly changed the lives of women in Wales. In 1939 the number of working women in the Principality was a little over 90,000. By 1945 that figure had risen to a staggering 200,000. The majority of those women were employed in the Royal Ordnance Factories in places like Glascoed, Rhigos and Bridgend. JOAN SMITH, MAISIE WILLIAMS and MYRTLE JENKINS remember the time with affection – and with a clear understanding of what it meant for women to suddenly find themselves valued and needed!

JOAN SMITH

I really do believe that a lot of women were liberated by the war. Women had been totally dependent on men before the war.

I remember a friend of mine whose mother went out to work. She helped clean a house. And my mother, although she worked very hard and kept lodgers, was quite superior about it. She said 'To go out charring!' I was amazed at that snobbery.

The men felt like it as well. They didn't want their wives out working because it took away their ability to maintain their home. When the war came all that went to the wall, it was all swept away.

I think, for the first time, women came into their own. During the war they were able to do all sorts of things. After the war they had no intention of going back to where they were before. They didn't want to be dependent.

They had their own money in their pockets and they could please themselves. A lot of the men who'd been away for five years or more – perhaps in the desert or somewhere – they came back to find that everything had changed.

MYRTLE JENKINS

I worked in the armaments factory up in Rhigos, near Hirwaun. I didn't particularly want to go there but I was called up. I went to the Unemployment people and asked if I could go in to the forces, thinking that I could be near my husband, wherever he was. But, no, they told me I was too old. I was twenty-one! And so I had to go to the factory.

The money was good if you were a piece worker. But I was on inspection, on the micrometers. I was trying to save for when Dai came home, trying to get something together for furniture and things. And I did.

It changed women's attitudes, working in the factory. You had to be more forceful – well, I mean, you were working with men as well as women. It was a case of standing up for yourself.

MAISIE WILLIAMS

It made a difference to you, working in the factory at Glascoed. You can pick out a narrow-minded person very easily and I often pat myself on the back and think, thank goodness I didn't turn out like that.

During the war thousands of women had served their country by working in the munitions factories. This photograph shows women from Dowlais, along with their male managers and foremen, at the Rhigos Munitions Factory.

DILYS CHAPMAN rose to a high position in British Telecommunications. She was given her big chance in the final years of the war, and in the immediate post-war period she rose rapidly through the ranks. Would she have achieved such a high position had it not been for the war?

DILYS CHAMPAN

> Possibly not. You really can't say how things would have gone. I was warned
> that some people, some of the engineers, might be difficult but I like to think
> that when it came out that I was going to be in charge of contracts, people
> were marvellous.
>
> A lot of our chaps went into the forces which left a gap, you see. And that's
> where women had to fill in – it's why I got the job in the first place. I suppose
> I would have got on, in the normal way, as a clerical person at Telecoms, but
> the war accelerated things.

After 1945 the need for armaments obviously declined and the armaments factories
were, generally, reduced to a care-and-maintenance standard. With men returning
from war service, many of the women who had filled in or taken over their jobs found
themselves out of work. In general, however, there did not seem to be much
resentment, although many of the women did miss the companionship of the factories.

LINDA WESTERMAN

> I left Glascoed just before the end of the war, once my baby was born. My
> father said 'You're not working down there with that TNT stuff. Pack it in
> now.' So I did, about three months before the baby was born.
>
> I missed it but there was nothing I could do about it. I just had to accept it.

MYRTLE JENKINS

> I finished at the factory in 1945. The war was over and a notice had been put
> up. What they were doing was dismissing all the girls – last on, first off, that
> was how it was.
>
> There was one young girl there. I knew she was an only child and lived with
> her mother, a widow. I said 'Look, is there any chance that I can go, because I
> don't want to stay. Can I go and let her stay?' And they agreed to that, so I
> came away.
>
> I was happy to leave. I was a dressmaker and that kind of work didn't suit
> me, machinery and all. A sewing machine I was used to, but ammunition and
> things? No, I didn't like it.

LINDA WESTERMAN

> It was good money in the factories, good money for those days. I suppose we
> were fetching home £10 to £12 a week. At the time it was more money than
> I'd ever seen.
>
> After the war a lot of women packed it in. They'd had enough but they all
> went and worked elsewhere. Apart from those who got married.

MAISIE WILLIAMS

> I don't think there was any resentment from the women, you know, about
> losing their jobs. When the men came back from the war they were given

priority, which was only right. If they could do without the women, men took their jobs but there wasn't any resentment.

Maybe it worked out that a woman was prepared to finish work or something had come up and she was ready to go. Perhaps she had young children or perhaps her husband was going to come into the factory and take her job. That was all right as there'd be a wage coming in. No, there was no resentment.

That sentiment is supported by men like ROY CHAPMAN who, after his discharge from the RAF, returned to work for British Telecommunications.

ROY CHAPMAN

I'd worked for British Telecommunications before the war and they'd kept my job open. They'd begun employing a lot of women, doing some of the jobs. And some of them became very good, fitting telephones and things. They were employed in the exchanges as well. That's how they made up the numbers.

When we came back, the women were found other jobs, often on the clerical side. I don't remember any resentment. That was just how it was.

For some women, however, the idea of going back to clerical work after years of being out in the open air and doing vitally important jobs was something they did not relish. The war had emancipated them – they could now work at jobs like tractor driving or as telephone engineers. Whatever they wanted to do, the opportunity was still there, even after the war. JOAN MACDONALD and DORIS CURTIS, both Land Army Girls, took very different paths.

JOAN MACDONALD

After I left the Land Army, I worked as a typist in a building firm for a few months. But then I left and bought an old Fordson tractor. I joined Ron, the grandson of the farm where I'd been in the Land Army, and he had a new Fordson Major. We contracted for other farms. We ploughed, sowed, mowed and were very busy.

One day the area that's now the museum at St Fagan needed ploughing. The Fordson Major got stuck so I pulled in front and Ron just hitched the chain on his tractor to the back of mine. And as he walked back to his Fordson Major, I pulled it out – along with the three-furrow plough. It was a wonderful machine, that Fordson.

DORIS CURTIS

I loved the Land Army but I was never tempted to do that sort of work again. When I came to Pembrokeshire to live I worked in a shoe shop and then I went to Lydstep Haven and worked in the office there.

The Land Army was hard work and I enjoyed it. But I didn't mind stopping. It wasn't like the munitions people where they were really earning good money. They'd have missed the money aspect of it, I think, but we didn't have much money in the Land Army. So it wasn't an issue.

After 1945 things were never the same again. The world had changed and women, while they might have lost their jobs in armament factories, were never again going to accept being relegated to secondary status.

JOAN SMITH

> Women who worked in the munitions factories, they earned jolly good money. And they began to have a social life which they could never have afforded before. Previously their husbands had kept them under – they'd held the purse strings. Now it was totally different.
>
> After the war it was a different sort of work, dress shops and things like that. Things opened up and luxury goods began to come in to the shops. So women found other sorts of work.

A changing world meant more adjustment but after six years of destruction and devastation it was something that most people were happy to accept.

The certificate sent by the Queen (later the Queen Mother) to mark the service of Joan MacDonald – Miss Joan Jenkins as she was then – in the Women's Land Army.

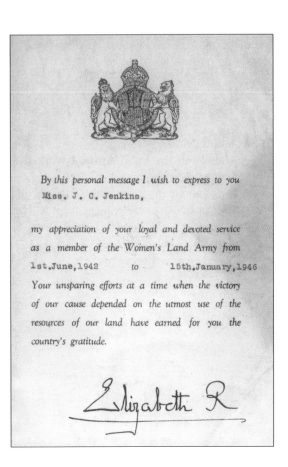

By this personal message I wish to express to you
Miss. J. C. Jenkins,

my appreciation of your loyal and devoted service
as a member of the Women's Land Army from
1st.June,1942   to   15th.January,1946
Your unsparing efforts at a time when the victory
of our cause depended on the utmost use of the
resources of our land have earned for you the
country's gratitude.

Elizabeth R

Chapter Four

A Brave New World

ONE OF the most important decisions to face any returning serviceman was the age-old dilemma that had always confronted warriors back from the wars – should they marry or continue with their bachelor existence? As the 'baby-boomer' generation can testify, huge numbers of marriages took place in the immediate post-war period and it was not long before babies followed in the wake of weddings.

Large numbers of soldiers, sailors and airmen had met their wives while in the services and that meant at least one of the pair would have to settle down in a new town or village. Other soldiers came home to rekindle pre-war relationships while many women who had been widowed during the war found happiness again with new partners who, themselves, could well be ex-servicemen.

The late CHARLIE STERRY met his wife Julia, a Sudeten German, while he was a prisoner of war. When he was repatriated he knew the relationship would be hard to maintain. He had been to the Czechoslovakian embassy, and was consulting with solicitors about how he could bring Julia out from behind the Iron Curtain, when he received an unexpected telephone call.

Charlie Sterry and his wife Julia in a photograph taken after she had journeyed many hundreds of miles across a shattered and war-torn Europe in order to be with him.

CHARLIE STERRY

Out of the blue she came over. She landed at Harwich and was befriended by an air-force officer. She had no money and he paid for her all the way to Paddington. She never had his name or anything. I would have like to have got in touch with that gentleman and thanked him.

Anyway, she ended up at Paddington, she couldn't go any further. So the police rang me and asked me if I would pay the fare for her to travel to Newport. That's what I did and met her at Newport station.

It was out of the blue. She couldn't speak a word of English. We got married in St Paul's Church on Sunday, 21st March, 1948. We had the reception in our sister's. She had a pub, the Mason's Arms, in Marshfield and we went down to look after it for six months. That's where my wife learned English.

Old Mr Lewis used to come in every dinnertime and sit on the bench outside. He'd have his pint and read to her. She'd have to read back to him and if she made a mistake he'd make her repeat it. That's how she learned English.

For most people, however, meeting future partners and marriage was much less dramatic, as ex-soldier GLYN MILLER recalls.

GLYN MILLER

We heard, myself and a number of friends, that the Inland Revenue were recruiting in Bridgend. Now I had applied for a place in a Training College, to train as a teacher, but I'd been told it would be a year before I could go. So I was looking for something to do for a year at least.

We all went along to the Income Tax and we were all taken on. There was a large room, full of ex-servicemen: air force, navy but mostly army. I worked there for about a year.

That's where I met my wife. I met her in the Income Tax office and we were married in March 1948.

For Land Army Girl DORIS CURTIS, the end of the war also brought marriage.

DORIS CURTIS

I met my husband Leslie just before the end of the war. He was working for the WARAG in a garage in Carmarthen. We used to take our vehicles there to be repaired and that's how I met him.

He'd been medically discharged from the army, around about 1944. He was certainly out of the army when I met him.

For widows, the end of the war was a traumatic affair. Peace had come but not for their loved ones. Sometimes, however, they were lucky enough to find new relationships, as LINDA WESTERMAN and SYLVIA BAILEY recall.

LINDA WESTERMAN

After my husband was killed I lived with my mother and father. Then the best man at my wedding – he was from Woolwich Arsenal like my husband and

working at Glascoed until he was called up – came back from the navy. He had
lodged with my mother and father during the war and when he came back he
wanted to come and live with them again. Well, come back he did.

About two years later we were married, in 1948. And he was a good
husband. He went back to work at the Royal Ordnance Factory and that's
where he worked until the day he died.

SYLVIA BAILEY

Some nice things did come out of the war because my mother was introduced
to somebody's friend who'd just come back from the war. And so my mum got
married again.

After being an only child for about ten years, I suddenly had a brother and a
sister – within two or three years of the war ending. So, yes, some nice things
do happen.

Deciding to get married was only the start – after that the problems began. DILYS
CHAPMAN was married to her husband Ron in 1947 and her first difficulty was to
arrange the wedding breakfast,

DILYS CHAPMAN

It was terrible, trying to organise that. We had it at home and my sisters were
wonderful. I mean, they were begging all sorts of things off people and the
neighbours were also very good. They'd bring in stuff for us.

We couldn't get a wedding cake but my sister had a Christmas cake and she
dolled that up a bit. You just couldn't get luxury things. Now, I was getting
married and I couldn't find a pair of silk stockings. Then, the night before the
wedding my sister came home and said 'Look what I've got – a pair of silk
stockings for your wedding.'

She was a manageress of a tobacconist next to the Queen's and she'd
mentioned it to a customer, probably somebody from Howells opposite. That's
how things went on, everybody helped out if they could.

After the wedding it was a case of trying to set up home. And in bomb-damaged
Wales that was not easy, particularly when most luxury goods seemed destined for
export.

BARBARA JONES

I was getting married, and putting a bottom drawer together but you couldn't
get nice china. Most of it was for export only. You could only buy this thick
earthenware in a hideous pink and green – awful!

Now and again, if you were lucky, you'd get some seconds. That was the
only way you'd get bone china. You might be lucky and get a cup that matched
a saucer. You'd get the cup, saucer and plate but you'd never get a full set.

There was a lovely shop in St Mary's Street – Carter's it was, a very long narrow shop, fascinating. Often you'd hear buzzes going around – 'Carter's, bone china.' You'd dash in and pick them over. Handle first, make sure there was no crack in the handle. There might be a tiny split somewhere, perhaps not right through. Or the pattern might not be right. But you'd grab them.

DILYS CHAPMAN

Bedding – you couldn't get linen. I remember mentioning it to a chappie who worked with me in the office. His mother had died and she was apparently stacked up with bedding. I was there one morning, grumbling, saying 'Oh it's terrible, I can't buy sheets and pillowcases.'

He said 'Well I might be able to help you out there.' And he brought in some sheets and pillowcases for me.

HUBERT 'BUZZER' REYNOLDS

It wasn't easy trying to set up a home after the war for the simple reason that the salaries you got were only about £3.10s a week. And out of that you had a family to see to; you had to provide food, furniture and pay the rent and rates. It was a difficult time, not just for me. Hundreds of others found it hard too. Wages weren't as good as they are today.

It was not just items of crockery and silk stockings that were in short supply. The basic requirements for a home – beds and tables and chairs – were equally as hard to find. And rationing was still in place for many items.

LINDA WESTERMAN

We didn't have a lot and what we had – with regards to getting a home together – was all this old utility stuff. You had to have so many units, like coupons. If you didn't have enough units, you couldn't have it. My mother used to say 'Don't bother – you can have this or that from this house.'

Mind you, if you went to a second-hand shop they didn't bother with units or coupons. It was laughable. Still, second hand was better than nothing – as long as it was clean.

GLYN MILLER

When my wife and I were first married, we rented furnished accommodation. We didn't get our own furniture until we had our own home. That was probably in 1949.

Furniture was available, utility furniture. I remember buying a bedroom suite and a dining-room suite from WHSmith of all people. An aunt of mine kept a little newsagents shop so she obviously had dealings with WHSmith and somehow she got us some sort of voucher. We went to Smith's warehouse in Cardiff and we bought these two suites. I remember that the dining suite was a lot better than the bedroom suite – that's long since gone. The dining-room suite still exists, I still have the sideboard.

When Labour won the election in 1945 they had promised a new and brighter future. It was a message that the people of Britain took to their hearts. Clement Atlee, the new Prime Minister, had said

> the general feeling was that they wanted a new start. We were looking towards the future. The Tories were looking towards the past.

Part of the new future had been neatly outlined in the Beveridge Report which was published in 1942, a few days after the battle of El Alamein. In many respects the report – a government document that sold a staggering 635,000 copies – was a championing of a better world, highlighting five significant problems that a post-war Britain should seek to abolish: Want, Disease, Ignorance, Squalor and Idleness.

In order to defeat these immense social problems, problems that had been the hallmark of the 1930s, Beveridge outlined a system of welfare that was built on three key elements – a free national health service, child allowances and full employment. The post-war Labour Government, with the mercurial Welshman Aneurin Bevan leading the way as Minister for Health, quickly began to put the Beveridge Report into action.

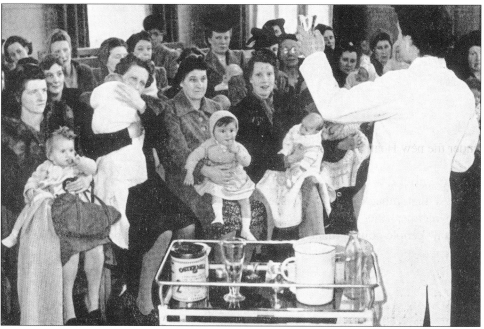

The National Health Service brought quality child care and many other benefits to the people of Wales.

It was not easy. Ideals are often very hard to translate into reality. Bevan's Welfare State, though in hindsight arguably flawed, became a shining beacon, a talisman for the new world. HARRY RADCLIFFE, then a miner in Nantymoel, remembers the time.

HARRY RADCLIFFE

I remember Nye Bevan: he announced and implemented the Welfare State. And we thought, as I say, God's Heaven. We didn't have to pay for the doctor's as we did before and during the war. We used to have to pay a penny a week into a special fund and we even paid another penny a week for our own ambulance.

But after the war, doctors, dentists, everything, all free. If you went to the doctor's surgery you didn't have to pay for prescriptions and things. I remember my sister-in-law, she had more teeth than she had cups of tea. She was changing them every fortnight. I suppose you could say people took advantage on that score. But it was a marvellous thing when you could go to the doctor's, free like that.

BARBARA JONES

I remember the Welfare State coming into being. I remember reading letters in the papers – usually from retired Colonels, people like that – saying we'd become a namby-pamby state, with people relying on the state too much. It shouldn't happen, they'd say, people won't want to work, they'd want the state to keep them.

RON SUMPTION

We had to register with a doctor. So my mother and myself, I remember, went up to the doctor's to do exactly that. I can remember my mother having free glasses under the National Health Service. Before the war you'd have had to pay for them.

As far as Barbara Jones is concerned, it was not just teeth and glasses that were free under the new Health Service.

BARBARA JONES

At that time, if you wore spectacles, they were free. Dentistry was free – which was nice. But wigs were also apparently free. Hairpieces. Suddenly you saw people going around in the most hideous wigs, men and women alike. You could tell from a distance – 'Oh, a wig!' I don't know why wigs were suddenly free but I suppose they thought they looked nice.

RON SUMPTION

I remember going to the dentist. The only dentist we'd gone to before was the school dentist. And the dentists in the Rhondda at that time, all they wanted to do was take your teeth out and give you a false set! So good dental care was most welcome.

Hospitals were revolutionised in this post-war period with modern buildings and modern equipment gradually being built or installed. In some cases it was slow progress, as EILUNED REES remembers.

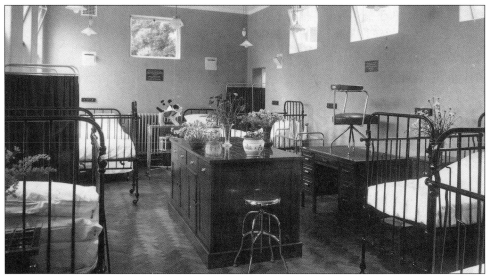

Hospitals were modernised and upgraded as part of the new Welfare State, which brought relief and comfort for many people.

EILUNED REES

> I had a goitre, a common occurrence in Wales at that time, and I was operated on when I was eighteen in Glangwilli Hospital, Carmarthen.
>
> Glangwili was the old army hospital and it was still army huts at that time. It was a marvellous hospital but nowadays it would be considered extremely basic. We were just in huts. So if you had to go down to another section to have a test, well, you'd be there all morning if it was raining. There were no corridors or anything – you just had to go out into the open air.

For people who were seriously ill or worked in dangerous jobs, the new National Health Service was a real boost.

HARRY RADCLIFFE

> Before the war you had to pay if you had an accident and had to go to hospital – you were charged for it. Okay, we paid into a special fund and they took the money out of that but you were still charged for it. And accidents were a regular occurrence in the mines.

Herbert Williams and Sylvia Bailey both have lasting memories of hospitals in this period.

HERBERT WILLIAMS

> We had a great deal to do with doctors in our family because we were plagued by chest problems. Two of my brothers had TB and I had it as well. One of my brothers actually died of TB, at home.

I was very healthy as a young child but rather sickly when I got into early adolescence. I was suspected of having TB – you know, shadows on the lungs – for a few years before I actually went into a TB sanatorium in Talgarth in 1948.

SYLVIA BAILEY

It must have been about two years after the end of the war – my mother had suffered with asthma all her life and then she was diagnosed as having TB. She had to go into a sanatorium.

The Health Service was very quick and got her into hospital; I think it was as much for our sake as hers. And it worked because none of us came down with TB.

HERBERT WILLIAMS

I went down to Talgarth in an ambulance. My mother came with me, all the way from Aberystwyth. I went into a ward, a four-bedder, and I was the youngest there. My mother went, leaving me there, obviously.

I got into bed and the guy in the bed opposite, he was a frizzy-haired guy – black frizzy hair – called Mal. He was a miner from Caerphilly. The screens were pulled back, after I'd got into bed, and he said 'How long did they say you were going to be in here, then?'

I said 'Oh six months.' He said 'You'll be effing lucky. Only dandruff cases get out in six months. You'll be lucky if you get out in two years.'

And they were prophetic words because I was there for two years. But it was a bit of a blow, then. It wasn't a very friendly introduction.

SYLVIA BAILEY

Mum was in a sanatorium just below Llandough Hospital near Dinas Powis. We used to go and visit her on a Saturday. I remember that she was in a ward and all along the one side were windows. And they were all open. It was freezing cold because it was wintertime.

As I say, we were allowed to visit on a Saturday. Not the little ones, just my dad and me. We'd walk up this long, long lane and when we got in we'd see all these ladies. They'd be in bed with their bedclothes almost up to their chins – with the windows wide open. It probably wasn't snowing but it was certainly all frosty and freezing cold. It was supposed to be good for them, fresh air. But it was quite laughable to see them.

HERBERT WILLIAMS

It was all fairly primitive, looking back. They were very well meaning but they had little to go on. There was no cure for TB in those days. It was just helping nature to take its own course, for good or ill. They had treatments such as the collapsing of lungs by injecting air between the plural walls – or more serious operations like hacking ribs away.

But mainly it was fresh air and rest. Those were the two prongs of treatment in the sanatorium.

The South Wales Sanatorium at Talgarth where Herbert Williams spent two years recovering from TB.

Despite the introduction of new drugs and new treatment regimes, it was hard not to get depressed at times.

HERBERT WILLIAMS

I was very homesick at first. If you go away from home at a young age you can, generally speaking, do things. You're involved with other people, you go out and enjoy yourself. But just being stuck there in bed all day?

And, remember, my brother had died a few months earlier. I can remember walking along the corridor one day, thinking 'I'm never going to come out of here. I'm going to be like Bobby. I'm going to die in here.'

There were times when I was very low and the mental state of people like me wasn't really taken into account. It was a very swift growing-up, a very curious circumstance. It was a kind of sentence but you didn't know how long you were sentenced for.

SYLVIA BAILEY

By the time my mum went into hospital, streptomycin was just coming in and they were carrying out trials. I can remember that – they wanted her to have certain things done to her. But I think by this time she was in her 40s and she wasn't very keen to have experiments, as she called them, done on her.

HERBERT WILLIAMS

There was a block just behind ours and there was a chap there, called Islwyn. He had TB Meningitis which was nearly always fatal. And these male orderlies, they said 'Oh the dog was howling all night outside Islwyn's. He's not going to last.'

Then we heard that a wonder drug was coming in from America – it was called streptomycin. It had never been tried before over here and they tried it out on Islwyn. And he got better – it was amazing, he actually survived TB Meningitis. He's still alive now, over eighty years old.

Herbert Williams and Sylvia Bailey's mother were lucky – they recovered. Such experiences did not affect most people in Wales but it was reassuring to know that the services were there if needed.

One thing that did have an effect on the people of Wales, however, was Child Allowance. Invariably made out in the woman's name, the allowance effectively put hard cash into the pockets of the people who did the direct caring!

GLYN MILLER

I remember we had Child Allowance in those post-war years. It wasn't for the first child, only for the second. My wife had a book with vouchers in it, one of which she tore out – every week, I guess. Or maybe the Post Office tore it out. I think she had about seven or eight shillings a week.

MAISIE WILLIAMS

We were given Child Allowance after the war. It was eight shillings a week but only for the second child. The first one, they just didn't want to know. You had nothing for the first child. I don't know why that was.

With so many houses destroyed during the war there was a very real housing shortage in the years after 1945. In 1944 the Temporary Housing Programme had promised a quarter of a million new houses but, in the event, just over 150,000 were actually built in the immediate post-war period.

One of the main thrusts of the programme was the creation of the famous prefab, prefabricated bungalows made mainly of wood. By 1948 nearly 125,000 of these supposedly temporary buildings had been erected, often on bombsites and wasteland. Designed to last just ten years, many prefabs were still in use in the 1980s – some are still lived in, even today (albeit with some degree of modification). They certainly did not deserve Nye Bevan's seething denouncement as

The prefab, for many newly-wed couples, was their first home together.

'rabbit hutches'. JOAN SMITH, GRACE NICHOLAS and GLENYS EDWARDS all lived in prefabs at this time.

JOAN SMITH

> I lived in a prefab for a while, for between six months and a year. They were quite comfortable. I suppose they were cold, but, then, we were always cold in those days – there was no central heating. And there were no wall-to-wall carpets, just lino and a few mats.

> But in the prefabs you had a bathroom which was very nice, because, those days, most people still bathed in front of the fire. And there was a little kitchen with a sink and things like that in it.

GRACE NICHOLAS

> They didn't look very good from the outside but inside we were absolutely thrilled because we had fitted kitchens and refrigerators and some form of central heating. We thought we were landed! I was living with my sister and when her husband came home from the war, they got a prefab.

> After I married, I moved into another prefab, one of my own. I must have been there for about twenty-five years. We had all the modern conveniences, things that most people in town didn't have, like bathrooms and separate toilets.

GLENYS EDWARDS

> I lived in a prefab for about four years. I loved it there. They were very compact, very easy to keep clean. We had a fridge, already put in for us, and a table which came down from the wall. It was a very friendly community there, in the prefabs. Everybody seemed to know everyone else.

> Do you know, I'd exchange my house today for a prefab if I had the chance.

Hubert 'Buzzer' Reynolds, a fireman in the post-war years, remembers the prefabs with affection – even though, professionally, he knew that they were a fire risk, being made essentially out of wood.

HUBERT 'BUZZER' REYNOLDS

> People were more careful then they are today. They were very fire-conscious and I can't even remember any serious fires taking place in a prefab. No, people were very careful.

> The prefabs were a wonderful invention. They had more in those little prefabs than most people had in their big houses. They had everything there, fridges, everything. It was all very compact.

SYLVIA BAILEY

> A friend of mine had a prefab in Gabalfa in Cardiff. I remember going in there and even though we lived in a house, this prefab was, to my mind, wonderful. It had a fridge and a built-in cooker. The whole of the kitchen was built-in,

actually, in those prefabs. And it had wardrobes. So you only needed a three-piece suite and a bed and you were there.

My friend, she was on her way. She was about twenty-four and she had her prefab, the first home of her own. I thought it was wonderful.

JOAN SMITH

The thing was, with a prefab, you could make it whatever you wanted. They were easy to clean after all those old-fashioned houses which had stone or wood floors. People liked living in the prefabs – they seemed to be a real community.

BARBARA JONES

Prefabs were very nice inside I heard but apparently they had a lot of condensation. But no, I thought they were lovely. They had a fitted kitchen. What I thought was absolutely marvellous was when you opened a cupboard door, down came an ironing board. I thought that was the height of mod cons.

They had cupboards. Up till then you'd have, maybe, a sink, a dresser. But the prefabs? I thought they were wonderful. Most people did.

Some prefabs have survived into the 21st century, even though they were intended to last for no more than ten years.

Modernisation has helped many prefabs to survive but, even today, there is no mistaking their essential design shape.

If you managed to find yourself a prefab you were lucky. For many newly married couples, there was no option but to rent rooms. Accommodation simply did not exist and, besides, buying or renting was an expensive business.

LINDA WESTERMAN

We lived at home for a while after we were married but then my husband said 'We'll get a place.' But, of course, the places weren't about. You just couldn't get a house or anything to rent.

ROY CHAPMAN

We'd always said it would snow when we got married and it did. We got married in January 1947. Then, of course, the problem was getting somewhere to live. One of the chaps I worked with, he was very good. He said he could let us have rooms in his house at Roath. We were there a few years and then went to live with my wife's sisters for a while, twelve months or so.

SYLVIA BAILEY

We lived in Mynachddu during most of the war and for a bit afterwards. My mum had relatives there and she always had rooms with them.

After she re-married we had a council house in Ely. And we had very little furniture. I can remember the carpets were just grey army blankets. That's how hard up my mum and dad were then.

LINDA WESTERMAN

We went down and put our names on the housing list, like you do, but there was nothing about. Then my husband said 'I'm going down to those tin places on the Polo Grounds.'

Corrugated-iron shacks or houses – all part of providing housing for bomb-damaged Wales.

They had, like, Nissan huts on the Polo Grounds and they were putting people in there. But my mother said 'You're not taking her down there.' And that was that knocked on the head.

There was an elderly lady living in the street and we knew her well. She called me one day and she said 'You can come and live in rooms here. It's only me in the house.' So that's what we did, we went and lived with her.

It took time but, gradually, things improved. Wages went up, more houses became available and standards of living improved. Yet for many, Labour's promise of a new world with a good life for everyone was far from being realised.

Once war was over, it was essential to get Britain back on her feet. There were jobs for everyone, even though wages were not particularly high.

One area where the Government had certainly made good its promises, however, was public ownership of key industries. The concept had been a central pillar in Labour's economic and social policies for years. And for those in the mining industry, nationalisation was like manna from heaven. The MP Emanuel Shinwell wrote that the transfer of the pits from private to public ownership was 'more than a technical and administrative change – it was largely psychological in character.' That was a viewpoint with which most miners would agree.

HARRY RADCLIFFE

We all knew it was coming – well, we were hoping. It had been part of the Labour manifesto, nationalisation of the coal mines. We were all for it – well, I mean, you'd have been daft not to be. The work underground was the same

but, how can I put it, you didn't have to salute any more. You respected the
manager, you respected him but you didn't have to say 'Yes, sir' or 'No, sir,'
all the time.

RON SUMPTION

I started work in September 1947. The pits were nationalised on 1st January,
1947. So I never worked for a private coal company but the nuances were still
there. I went into the Scientific Department, the Coal Board Laboratory in
Treorchy, because I was interested in chemistry at that time – you know what
schoolboys are like.

HARRY RADCLIFFE

Once we had nationalisation we had different machinery, we had cap lights,
better lighting, better facilities. We even had a pithead bath that we didn't have
to pay for, once nationalisation came. We'd had to pay a shilling a week just to
bath at the pithead baths up till then.

Nationalisation was a big thing for the miners. We all accepted it and took
the benefits that came with it. I went onto a Deputies' course and became a
Deputy. That's what I remained for the rest of my working days.

Nationalisation of the coal mines came in 1947. It brought new working conditions and a better
quality of life for all miners.

RON SUMPTION

> There were vast expectations on the part of the miners. It was now their pit, you know? And nobody else's.
>
> My own personal view is that the big problem was the miners thought that the coal, the pits, had been nationalised for their benefit rather than for the benefit of the country. That was a big flaw in all nationalisations.
>
> Mind you, it was incumbent on the Coal Board to be a much better employer than the private owners. And, in general, I think they were.

Demobilisation affected the mines as well as the armed forces. Bevin Boys were discharged in exactly the same way as soldiers. As HARVEY ALFORD remembers it, however, they had something of a raw deal when compared to those serving in the army.

HARVEY ALFORD

> Yes, I think we did have a raw deal. If you were in the forces you had a demob suit when you finished. We didn't have anything like that. They just said 'Thank you very much, good morning, on your way.' I think I had a free pass to go home but that was about all.

For those who remained working underground, however, there was a great improvement in working conditions after 1947.

HARRY RADCLIFFE

> Many things, like facilities, became better. The machinery was better and safety appliances came in. Under the NCB it was really good. We didn't even have hard hats till after the war. We had little Dai caps and if you hit your head, you either got a cut or a sore head. A lot of serious head injuries could have been saved if we'd had hard hats.
>
> I remember one time, after nationalisation, I was attending a big fall. And I was up in this hole, with the men, showing them what I wanted done and a big stone came and hit me on the head. If I hadn't had a hard hat on, I wouldn't be here now.
>
> The NCB also provided gloves, provided everything. We just had to accept it.

RON SUMPTION

> I think one of the most significant things about nationalisation was the introduction of the Ladder System. Anybody in the National Coal Board could apply for further education and, consequently, it expanded the Technical Colleges in South Wales at that time. People did their Higher National Certificates in electronics, mechanics and chemistry.
>
> There were a few Schools of Mines scattered around the South Wales Coalfield – one at Crumlin, one down in Swansea and then Treforest. A lot of people tried it. There was a big drop-out but those people who stuck at it did very well.

And, of course, the knock-on effect, ultimately, when it came to the 1960s, was that steelworks like Llanwern and Margam were literally staffed by electricians or mechanics or fitters from the Coal Board.

HARRY RADCLIFFE

It was a hard life, underground, particularly up until 1947-48. After that, machinery came in and there was different organisation. They took all the horses away, for a start. I would say, towards the end, it was easier for miners.

To start with we worked with pick and shovel, sledge and wedge. I used a curling box which I had bought from the old Gwalia Stores – you had to put the coal into this curling box because they didn't want dirt in it. You weren't allowed to shovel it – if a manager or official caught you doing that you'd get a boot up the arse!

But things improved after nationalisation. I don't think we'd have had the pits so long if it hadn't been for nationalisation. The pits just wouldn't have gone on that long.

RON SUMPTION

It's impossible to picture the topography of the valleys without the mines. When you look at the Rhondda, the only area a pit occupied was a couple of hundred yards square. But underground, running out from the shafts, you would have as many as two or three thousand people working.

There were always accidents in the pits but I never saw one myself. They became much more safety-conscious once the Coal Board came about.

Mining was only one of the several industries nationalised in the post-war period, the railways and the steel industry being two other major organisations to come into public ownership.

The railways were also a target for nationalisation under the new Labour Government

Education had been state controlled since 1870 but the 1944 Education Act revolutionised the schooling process. By the terms of the Act, the school-leaving age was raised to fifteen – its implementation being delayed until 1947 – and was to be raised again to sixteen, as soon as it became practicable.

The outstanding feature of the Act, however, was that for the first time in British history, all children aged between eleven and fifteen were to pass through some type of secondary education – previously they could have remained in the primary sector. Additional schools (and larger ones) meant that more teachers were urgently needed.

To meet the post-war demand for extra teachers, emergency training colleges were opened, offering one-year courses for men and women who might want to come into the teaching profession. Many of them, because army service had interfered with their education, had lower academic qualifications than were normally required. However, whatever the candidates lacked in the way of paper qualifications, they more than made up the deficit with their experience and enthusiasm.

GLYN MILLER and JACK CARRADICE were two ex-soldiers who decided to try their hand at teaching.

GLYN MILLER

I went to college in Cardiff. It was at the old American army barracks at the bottom of Allensbank Road in the Heath. The course lasted about fourteen months, I think, and was very intense. We didn't have holidays on the usual scale. We had, perhaps, a week at Christmas and a week in the summer. As I say, it was very intensive but it seemed to work.

JACK CARRADICE

I wanted to do something with my life. I'd always been good at art and so I thought, maybe I'd become an art teacher.

The emergency training scheme was hard. I was away from my family, in these old army huts on the Heath in Cardiff. I used to get home at weekends but money was short because I was trying to keep a wife and child back home. I was lucky, they were living with Mary's parents, otherwise we'd never have managed.

GLYN MILLER

Those of us who lived close by were expected to travel daily. I'd catch the 7.20 Western Welsh bus into Cardiff and a tram up to the corner of Allensbank Road and then walk the rest of the way.

It was largely lectures but we did have, I think, three periods of teaching practice.

JACK CARRADICE

The course was pretty intensive, with lectures and tutorials, but because I was taking art, I did get out from College once in a while for sketching practice. I remember once being set to draw a railway viaduct that ran across one of the valleys. But what I drew, quite frankly, owed more to my days up in the north of England than it did to my brief visit to the Rhondda.

GLYN MILLER

For teaching practice we were sent to schools fairly near our homes. I had one spell in a Secondary Modern school in Bridgend. The Secondary Modern schools were a post-war thing. And they were good schools – there was some very good work done there. Students from some of the Secondary Moderns went on to University.

JACK CARRADICE

It was a funny time, looking back. Money was tight so I used to go to the old outdoor café in the Hayes and order beans on toast. Then I'd eat the beans one at a time – I even cut some of them in half to make them last longer. I don't know it if worked but I do remember people looking at me as if I was mad.

The sketch drawn by Jack Carradice during his Emergency Training in Cardiff. It captures the atmosphere of industrial Wales in the immediate post-war years but, really, owed as much to the manufacturing areas of North England as it did to the Welsh valleys.

Another time, I had this beautiful brown jumper Mary had knitted for me. It had a big collar and in the winter I wore it under my jacket with the collar outside. One day the Principal came past me in the Common Room. He stopped, stared, then reached over and pushed the jumper collar under my jacket. 'Teaching is a profession for gentlemen, Mr Carradice,' he said. 'Gentlemen wear their collars inside their jackets.' Then he wandered away in a cloud of pipe smoke. I think that was the only time he ever spoke to me.

The 1944 Education Act had created what was known as the tripartite system – a layer of three different types of secondary school, Grammar, Secondary Modern and Technical. Selection suddenly became important. The system had been planned in order to provide the education that best suited each individual child but, in practice, parents soon became desperate to see their children placed in what they regarded as the 'top school' – the Grammar School. ROBERT NISBET became a teacher and remembers the hated eleven-plus exam from both sides, as a teacher and pupil.

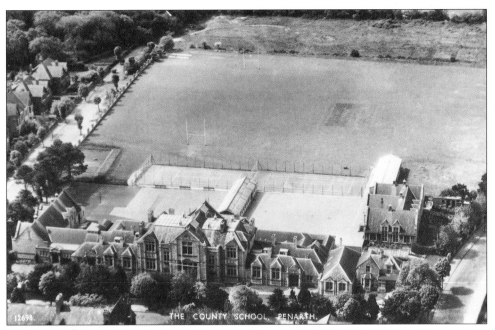

The County School at Penarth, soon to become a Grammar School under the Labour Government's new Tripartite System.

ROBERT NISBET

> You got to Grammar School after an eleven-plus exam. That was rigorously in place very early on. I remember, in my primary school, there was talk of a 'Prelim' and a 'Scholarship'. The schools would do their own preliminary sifting of the pupils for the scholarship exam.
>
> I can recall a lot of stress and unhappiness brought to a lot of children by this very strict, very severe system. We talk now of SATS and the stress they cause children but that's nothing like the stress from this rigid system that, in many people's eyes, meant failure for some at the age of eleven. It was pretty grim.

JACK CARRADICE

> I went to teach in one of the new Secondary Moderns. It was rough and tough in those early days. I don't think the schools had quite sorted out their role and purpose at that stage. Anyway, I had this class of disinterested youngsters to take for Games.

'Can we play our soccer game, sir?' they asked. I agreed, not really knowing what they had in mind. And their game consisted of a player holding his hand against a pebble-dash wall while the rest of the class took pot shots at it. Nobody ever moved their hand, that would have been unthinkable but squashed and mangled fingers were the order of the day. We never played that particular game again.

Newly qualified teacher Jack Carradice enjoying the long summer break!

ROBERT NISBET

The whole curriculum in primary school was usually geared to English, Maths and Intelligence – which, for some reason, was what the Eleven Plus tested you in. I remember, once, somebody saying that his daughter was good in English and Maths but not so good in Intelligence – a pretty frightening thought!

I think I was lucky because in my primary school we had a teacher called Billy Childs. He was a wonderful teacher who encouraged us to feel that we were in school to learn things like History and Geography. We never felt stressed or impelled towards that Eleven Plus, even though we all knew it was there.

Like many Welshmen, Glyn Miller had to leave the country of his birth in order to start teaching. It was several years before he was able to take up a job in Wales.

GLYN MILLER

I had to move out of Wales for my first teaching job and started my career in Birmingham. It wasn't an affluent part of the city and practically every suburb had a shop called 'Cheval Meat Store'. On the plate outside the window, as a subtitle, it said 'Horse Meat for Human Consumption'. I remember a colleague going over to the store opposite the school and asking for meat for her dog. The manager was most angry with her. He said 'We don't sell dog meat. We sell horse meat for human consumption.' And he wouldn't serve her.

In the years after 1945, there was much hardship and, at times, people wondered if Britain had actually won the war. It took time and strength of character but, slowly, surely, the foundations of modern society were laid.

Chapter Five

Work, Rest and Play

PEOPLE WORKED hard in the post-war years. It was something that had to be done if Britain was to claw its way back into a position of economic strength and power. While the immediate aim was to get people working again, rebuilding the country and producing materials for export – which, in turn, would bring in much needed revenue – there was also time for a little entertainment.

LESLIE GRIFFITHS, NESTA MILLER and GRACE NICHOLAS all had first-hand experience of working conditions in those immediate post-war years in the town of Pembroke Dock.

LESLIE GRIFFITHS

Before the war I was in the building trade, before I went into the army. I came out early under what they called Class B. It was specially for building trade workers – to come back early and rebuild all the bombed-out towns. And you know, I still haven't been properly demobbed, just the Class B get-out.

I went up to Shrewsbury to get the suit, the hat, everything. And outside there were these spivs. They'd give you £5 for the box – your demob suit was in a cardboard box. I didn't sell mine – it was the first suit I'd ever had.

NESTA MILLER

My husband was on the Sunderlands during the war, on aircrew. After the war he came back to Pembroke Dock and got a job. And then he went into business for himself, a workshop in Water Street. Water Street Coachworks. He was a marvellous panel beater.

We got married in 1945 – they actually dropped the Atom Bomb when I was on my honeymoon! It was strange coming back to Pembroke Dock but we made a life here. Bill found work easy enough and then opened his own business. Oh, Billy Miller made a life for himself.

GRACE NICHOLAS

The Local Council was trying to attract industry to the area and this handkerchief factory was set up in Pembroke, in the Town Hall. It was small – they only employed about a hundred people, making these handkerchiefs for sale abroad. You were encouraged to make things for export in those days and so we sent packets of handkerchiefs all over the world.

LESLIE GRIFFITHS

> When I came out of the army, I went back into the building trade, repairing all the houses in the town. I don't think there's a house in Pembroke Dock that I haven't been into, either inside or on the roof – mostly on the roofs, re-slating.
>
> The first job we did was re-build Tom Bowling's place in Commercial Row. That had been bombed to the ground and we re-built that. It was the first time we'd used concrete blocks for a building.
>
> It took, I reckon, about ten years to make Pembroke Dock look reasonable again. Well, it took three years just to put all the roofs back on.

Leslie Griffiths (left), and colleagues, shortly after his early demob in order to help rebuild the bomb-damaged towns of Wales.

Entertainment in Wales for adults and children alike at that time tended to be rather 'home-spun'. There were few ready-made entertainments, as Doris Curtis and Marco Carini remember.

DORIS CURTIS

> My husband, Les, he was a bell-ringer. The Curtis family came from Newbury and they were all bell-ringers – Leslie's father and brother and Leslie himself. They used to say the Curtis family could get two sets of ringers, there were so many of them. So I started bell-ringing too, in St Peter's in Carmarthen.
>
> We used to go off on weekends, you know, to various towers, bell-ringing. It was more or less the only social life we had in those days.

MARCO CARINI

You made your own fun in those days. When I was young, in the summer, we had a tent up on the old bit of ground out the back. The girls would all be there, pretending to cook.

You played all sorts of games like 'Kick the Can' and 'Cannon'. And 'Granny in the Night' – when it was dark you'd get a scarf, wind it up into a knot and whoever was granny he'd chase you. If he hit you with that, you'd know you'd been hit.

There was hopscotch and bowlies – you couldn't buy a bowlie, you'd make them out of the rims of buckets or barrels. You'd run down the road with them, going along like a wheel – hours of fun.

For older teenagers and for adults, however, entertainment tended to revolve around the dance halls and cinemas.

SYLVIA BAILEY

We all belonged to concert parties. We'd always be having these concerts and there always seemed to be parties going on. I used to have a reasonably good voice and I used to be a soloist.

But, really, it was dancing. Oh, I loved my dancing. You had to be, I think, fifteen to go into these dances at places like the Regal and the Pavlova but I usually managed to get in. I had dancing lessons because I loved dancing so much.

There would be a five-piece band wherever you went. They weren't anyone in particular but they were always very, very good. Jiving was the main thing then.

BARBARA JONES

I suppose you'd spend a lot of time with friends, at friends' houses. You'd get to the cinema a couple of times a week but dancing was the most popular thing, I think.

We'd go to the Regal – or to City Hall. It was always ballroom dancing, really enjoyable.

SYLVIA BAILEY

The Regal was at the top of Western Avenue and the Pavlova was in Canton. And the City Hall? Well. You were really elevated when you went to the City Hall.

EILUNED REES

I loved going to the pictures – we all loved going to the pictures. We'd go as a crowd and we must have looked beautiful. Imagine a group of children, all eleven or twelve, all wearing identical Fair Isle caps and gloves because there'd only be one pattern in the village. All different coloured wool maybe but we'd still be dressed up the same, sitting in a row in the pictures.

I loved the *Robin Hood* films and *The Three Musketeers*. Or *Just William* – anything really. It didn't matter what the film was, it was just escapism.

The cinema was probably the main form of entertainment in the post-war years. Every town and almost every suburb of places like Cardiff and Swansea had its own picture house. Some, like the Monico in Rhiwbina, Cardiff, were very elegant affairs, almost works of art in their own right. (Photograph taken in 2003 by Janet Salter before the cinema was closed.)

BARBARA JONES

We went to all the films – Clark Gable, Ray Milland, Van Johnson. I couldn't understand why people went mad about them, couldn't understand why they were put in those romantic roles. They were old men to us – even Clark Gable. He should have been a father! And then there was Betty Grable, Lauren Bacall, all of them.

HARRY RADCLIFFE

We had lots of picture houses in the valley, in the Workmen's Halls for a start. There was one in Ogmore Vale, then there was the Olympia which has been pulled down now – well, it fell down because the river undermined it.

The cinemas were always full – all the back seats, that's where we were! In the winter, when I was courting, we'd go every night – Monday in Nantymoel, Tuesday at Ogmore Hall, Lymp on a Wednesday. Then they changed the films so it was back up at Natymoel again.

JOAN SMITH

The only entertainment in Pembroke – apart from a few dances in places like the Drill Hall – was Haggars Cinema. There was a cinema in Pembroke Dock but transport was difficult.

I remember one night I couldn't get on the bus back from Pembroke Dock. I'd left my friends as they lived in Pembroke Dock and it was a long, lonely walk back. There was this fellow I knew slightly – he was going out with a girl I

worked with. He said 'I'll walk you home across Bird Cage Walk.' It was a short
cut and I was very grateful because somebody had been murdered along there.

Sometimes cinemas were little more than iron sheds, albeit with a brick or stone porch – practical in
the extreme. This shows the Grand Cinema – the name belies its appearance – in Pembroke Dock, just
before its demolition.

VALERIE CARINI and ROBERT NISBET remember the Saturday morning
performances that most cinemas put on for young children in those early post-war
days.

VALERIE CARINI

I loved the pictures, really loved them. When we were very young we used to
go to the Saturday morning shows. That's when you were about nine or ten.
Our parents would let us go because it was in the morning. It was wonderful:
all sorts of different things on the screen, and the music playing. Wonderful!

ROBERT NISBET

The Saturday morning cinema clubs thrived at about this time. You'd get
various bits of advert and a cartoon to start. Then a main feature film – I can't
remember much about them. But I can remember the serials – the *Superman*
serials seemed to go on endlessly, year after year. I remember some of the
villains, they were usually Japanese – very little political correctness in film-
making in those days.

VALERIE CARINI

After you came out of the pictures, you'd have a look around Woolworths.
You'd buy something there and then go home.

ROBERT NISBET

> I remember this shout which I can only describe as a sort of 'Yeay!' – as if we
> were starting to shout 'Yes' and then changed it to 'Hurray', halfway through.
> And this shriek, these shrill boy's voices, went up every time the villain got a
> sock on the jaw. It was passionate, film-going, in those days shortly after the
> end of the war.

VALERIE CARINI

> When we were a bit older, then we'd still go to the pictures. There'd be a first
> house and second house. I always remember, one day, we saw the start of the
> second house – after being there for the first – and my mother was going to
> send for the police because we were late coming home.
>
> I always remember that, I think the film was *Miranda* or something like
> that. Oh, it was wonderful, the pictures! We loved it.
>
> Favourite stars? Oh the musicals, all those dancers, all those singers.
> Deanna Durbin, I used to love her.

Sometimes, perhaps once or twice a year, the towns of Wales were visited by fairs or
possibly even by a circus. And ROBERT NISBET remembers the excitement of all
small boys when the fair came around.

ROBERT NISBET

> I remember Portfield Fair and the smaller May Fair. They were very popular
> because they loomed in the year as one of the very few highlights that were not
> of our own making. They were like Christmas, the fairs, with all the
> razzmatazz and ersatz music – a real thrill.

Street fairs with their dodgem cars, roundabouts and stalls brought entertainment to the Welsh towns,
places that had been starved of such entertainment for years.

I can remember saving five shillings to go to the fair and going up on the Octopus, tilting backwards in the thing and four shillings and nine pence dropped out of my pocket onto the ground below.

You had dodgem cars, the Swirls, everything. Of course, if you look back to those years just after the war, there were things you wouldn't get in more politically-correct times. First of all there was a Wall of Death which must have been incredibly dangerous as motorbikes rocketed up to the heights while the spectators – small boys among them – leaned over, watching. That must have been so dangerous.

As he got older ROBERT NISBET, like most boys in South Wales, gradually found other pleasures at the fair.

ROBERT NISBET

There was a boxing booth where people were pounded nightly – usually the spectators. They'd pay, I seem to remember, a pound if somebody lasted a round with one of their hired toughs. Of course they never did – I think it was old John Barleycorn they were taking on.

There was also a striptease. There would be a very discreet model and crowds of Pembrokeshire farmers baying out general criticism. I remember once, a crowd of us managed to get into the striptease and were looking on, rather bemusedly. In the midst of all this there was shout from one of the farmers, 'Mind that wasp!'

The model, as if to make up for her earlier discretion, produced one pose – full backside nude. Shouts of approval went up, shouts of 'That's the game.' And in the middle of it came 'There's that bloody wasp again!'

For boys like ROBERT NISBET, the arrival of a circus was a very special treat in the tiny West Wales town of Haverfordwest.

ROBERT NISBET

There were circuses coming round from shortly after the end of the war. I remember talking to someone when I was in Infants School and he'd been to the circus on the first night – there were three nights of it. We were due to go, the whole family, on the second night.

In the playground boys were retelling the clown's jokes. You

Robert Nisbet (right) and friends enjoy a day on the river. It was a time when, for children, playing outdoors seemed to occupy most of their time.

look back now and realize these jokes may not have been exactly in the Bob
Hope class. It turned out that the clown had called somebody 'a silly sausage'.
And that verbal gem was repeated for the whole day at school.

Fêtes and carnivals were also very popular in the immediate post-war years. They
involved the whole community and were relatively cheap to put on. After all, most
groups could get hold of a lorry – and, sometimes, it didn't need even that, as
MARCO CARINI, GRACE NICHOLAS and JOYCE LLOYD remember.

MARCO CARINI

There were carnivals every year after the war. Even in Beaufort with its big
hill, they always had a carnival. We used to end up down on the Recreation
Ground and, in those days, my father would take the ice cream out of the
freezer in the shop. He'd have two men to help him carry it down. And when it
was gone, it was gone. He didn't have a freezer to put it in down there. He'd
have enough dry ice around it to get it down there but that was it. He took
more money down there than he would in the shop all day.

All the carnivals had lorries off the coalmen – they'd have awful trouble
coming up the hill. Once I took part in a carnival in Ebbw Vale. The Beaufort
Bombshell we called our float. We made a kind of car out of a sidecar and
motorcycle and we won first prize. At that time they were doing stock-car
racing down in Neath and that's where the idea came from.

The Beaufort Bombshell – Marco Carini (inside the sidecar) and John Wintle win first prize in the
Ebbw Vale carnival.

GRACE NICHOLAS

We always used to take part in the local carnival, entering floats. I came back to Pembroke Dock from Plymouth just after the war and could never understand why there wasn't a bridge across the Cleddau River. So we set up this float, asking for a bridge – the Cleddau Bridge. But that didn't come in for another fifteen or so years.

JOYCE LLOYD

The carnivals? Well, we had floats. We had one called the Blue and White Minstrels. Once we built one for the World YMCA and we all dressed up as different countries on the float. We won first prize for that, a prize of £7. And we sent that off to the World YMCA.

However, one of the most popular forms of entertainment in these pre-television days was wireless.

EILUNED REES

There were some things you never missed, like the News or ITMA (*It's That Man Again*). I used to rush home to hear the News even though I never understood it all.

We had to take our batteries to the old mill to be recharged. It was up a very steep hill and I'd be carrying batteries full of acid up that hill just in order to listen to *Dick Barton, Special Agent* or something like that.

As MILLIE JOHN remembers, sometimes radio programmes that came on the wire, through a relay, could cause more than a few difficulties.

MILLIE JOHN

Our radio was on a relay – it went to all the houses in town. And my husband thought he'd be clever. He put a switch on the wall, to switch our wireless on and off, to save getting up.

My next door neighbour, she said 'Millie, I can only get certain programmes.' And I said 'Well, you go in the house and I'll switch my radio on'. And she did and she said 'It's come on.' I switched mine off and she said 'It's gone off again.' The switch my husband had put in was turning her radio on and off along with mine.

JOAN SMITH

We all used to pack into somebody's house to listen to *Children's Hour*. Not a word would be spoken. We were all absolutely fascinated. *Children's Hour* was always on at five o'clock.

EILUNED REES

We'd listen to music as well. My first great acquaintance with music came from the music programmes on the radio. Yes, my generation will always be hooked on the radio. It was very much a part of our lives.

For most people, reading books was also essential. During the war, civilians and soldiers had avidly devoured whatever reading material the publishers could put out – and once peace came, the pastime did not go away.

EILUNED REES

I read avidly. We had boxes of library books delivered to our school, big wooden boxes. There was no limit to the number of books you could take home. I remember staggering along with as many as I could carry. My friends and I would swap our books after we'd read them.

JACK CARRADICE

Everybody read in those days. Paperback books were relatively cheap and you always swapped or passed on anything you'd read. Remember, in the evenings there was only radio and reading was a great alternative. If people didn't read books they always read the newspaper.

EIULNED REES

I read anything I could lay my hands on, anything at all. My father was a great reader and I'd read books from his bookcase. I suppose I read things that were totally unsuitable for a child. I remember our doctor calling and being absolutely amazed to find me reading Walter Scott – a child of eleven ploughing through them all.

The newspaper was also very important. Unlike now, we had tremendous faith in newspapers. I remember the saying would be 'But I saw it with my own two eyes, there in black and white.' We believed everything we read. I think journalists were pretty honest at that time. After all, we'd been through a terrible crisis, they weren't going to muck around with news anymore. Things were too serious to be played with.

For many people, however, entertainment or leisure activity meant sport, watching it and playing it. The Welsh had always been a sporting nation, revelling in the success of village, town and national sides. Rugby and soccer were particularly popular but, in these immediate post-war years, the range of sports available was remarkably wide.

RON SUMPTION

The valleys of Wales were vibrant places in those days. I loved sport and played rugby for my Grammar School. The thing about the Rhondda, it's such a very competitive area as far as sport's concerned because there are always so many local derbies.

Take the rugby in the Grammar Schools. There were five Grammar Schools in the Rhondda so you'd have ten local derbies every year. It was the same with the villages, with all their rugby and soccer sides.

LESLIE GRIFFITHS

Ivor Cole and me, we were the instigators who founded Pennar Robins football club. We had a meeting in Victory Hall in Pennar and the positions were all given out, secretary, sidesmen and so on. And that was it, Pennar Robins football club was founded on June 30th, 1946. The club's still going.

Conditions were not always easy in those years. Players shared tin baths after the matches while showers and a regular supply of hot water lay many years in the future. Sometimes even the games themselves came under threat.

LESLIE GRIFFITHS

We used to play on what we called Big Field. During one particular match there was a lot of action around the goal. Everyone was very excited. And then along came this tractor, driven by Dennis Butland. He had orders to plough the land to grow food for the home market. He went right across the field as we played.

We were shocked but we kept on playing. Dennis was going round and round us, as the game went on. In the end we had to pack it in though. That was the end of that field for soccer.

RON SUMPTION

The Rhondda had quite a few Boys' Clubs. And you'd go there and play table tennis and snooker. Treorchy was also a good tennis centre – they had seven grass courts and three red-ash courts. And there was a good cricket pitch there, too.

For HARRY RADCLIFFE there was only one sport – cycling. He had been riding bicycles since before the war, thinking nothing about coming up from his shift in the mines and setting off for a 30-mile trip down the valley. After the war finished, like many other miners, he had the opportunity to really develop his sport.

HARRY RADCLIFFE

I'd be off every night, doing 20 to 30 miles, on a trip down to Ogmore-by-Sea or Southerndown. And then on weekends, we'd be racing on the Sunday morning. Some Saturdays we'd be off to Bristol. We'd meet by Ogmore Cemetery, say by half past three, and cycle to Newport.

We'd find out, then, if the ferry was going, from Beachley to Aust. It if was we'd catch it. But if not we'd go by train. We'd race 25 or 30 miles in the morning and then cycle home. Then off to work the next day. That was our life then.

Harry Radcliffe prepares for a long-distance bike ride.

The 1948 Olympic Games were held in London and with world-class cyclists competing at Herne Hill it was too good a chance to miss for Harry Radcliffe and his wife.

HARRY RADCLIFFE

My wife and I knew, back in 1945-46, that the Olympics were coming so we started saving. We put half a crown a week away and when the time came my wife and I – and another partner and his wife – cycled up to London to watch.

Two weeks we were there, going to the races most days. We saw Reg Harries, our leading cyclist in those days, miss out on a gold medal by half an inch. They didn't have photo finishes in those days but it was really close. And you should have seen the women crying after that.

It was a great experience, to be there to see the Olympic Games.

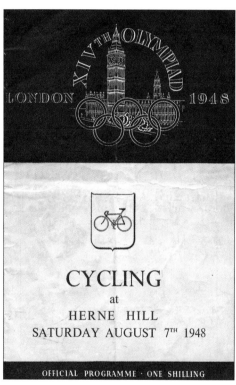

The Olympic Games came to Britain in 1948 – two programmes kept by Harry Radcliffe mark the cycling events at Herne Hill.

Cycling was extremely popular in the mining areas at this time – and yet it was not exactly a cheap hobby.

HARRY RADCLIFFE

The best bike of all, the Raleigh Record Ace, cost me about twelve guineas. I was putting half a crown a week to one side to pay for that bike – a lot of money in those days. It was a full day's work to put on a bike.

Mind you, cycling was our life. On Sundays there would be anything between 30 and 40 bikes going off for a ride, the whole road full of them. When you think of the bikes they use today it makes you envious. Some of us were racing on 2-inch tyres and 26-inch wheels. Those tyres would be as thick as your thumb.

Golf had always been a sport for the upper classes. There had been a number of artisan clubs – or artisan sections of well-established clubs – in South Wales during the 1920s and 1930s but, in general, the game was really the preserve of the moneyed classes. After the end of the Second World War, however, things began to change. Golf Clubs needed new blood, new members, and age-old class differences began to break down in the wake of the war that had been fought to defeat tyranny. In effect, the game of golf became available to all sections of society.

DENIS MORGAN served in the desert with the Eighth Army during the war. When he returned to South Wales after his demob he decided that he would like to try his hand at golf. It was a game he had already dabbled with – very briefly.

DENIS MORGAN

My wife became a member of Llantrisant and Pontyclun Golf Club when I was away in the army – a friend of hers was playing, so she became a member too. I came home on embarkation leave and thought I'd go round with them. It was my first taste of golf and I thoroughly enjoyed it. I borrowed their clubs, of course, and really loved it. It was only that once, about 1940 I think, but I thoroughly enjoyed the game.

When he was demobbed in 1946, Denis Morgan decided to join Llantrisant and Pontyclun. He became a member in March 1946.

DENIS MORGAN

There was a competition on the August Bank Holiday, three months later, and I won it. I won a tankard. There were one or two people who objected – 'He played in the war,' they said. But all I'd had was this one game, as a guest.

It wasn't easy to gain acceptance at first but, in time, Denis was made to feel more than at home.

DENIS MORGAN

When I joined it was rather early and some of them were a bit toffee-nosed. But after a year or so everybody was welcomed, everybody was so friendly. It's a very friendly club now – always has been.

Living alongside the golf course brought quite a few benefits.

DENIS MORGAN

I often played on my own in those early days. I'd jump over the fence and play a couple of holes before going to work in the morning. Later I played for the club first and second teams and was one of the founder members of the Seniors' Section. My wife, my two sons and my daughter (for a while), we all played. Golf was my life after the war. My wife and I played a lot together. It was a real pleasure.

One major change that came about in the post-war period was the advent of paid holidays. This was particularly the case in the mining industry where the phenomenon of Miners' Fortnight quickly established itself as a tradition in the years after nationalisation. Yet it was not just miners who now began to take regular holidays. All spectrums of society began to look forward to the annual two-week break – they had worked for it and they were going to enjoy it.

In the immediate post-war years, dozens of caravan parks were created in order to cater for the large numbers of holidaymakers who, thanks to things like Miners' Fortnight, were now able to take an annual break.

DORIS CURTIS

I always wanted to go home for our holidays, back to Lancashire. So that's what we did. I remember one trip in particular. My father was very ill and there were no trains running because it was that terrible winter of 1947. But I insisted on going home.

We drove all through the night. It was a horrible journey with us digging ourselves out from snowdrifts all the time.

After my mother and father died, we used to go to Newbury, every year, for holidays. We used to go there for weekends as well but it wasn't as easy to get to in those days. Not like it is now.

MARCO CARINI

My mother and father, every now and then, used to go back to Italy for a holiday. Before the war they'd taken my other brothers but I'd always stayed at home.

Then, in 1947 when I was eleven, my mother and father, my younger brother and me, the four of us went out to Italy on the train. We caught the train at Newport and went right the way through to Italy. We stayed for a month at my father's home, Chieaza Bianco near Bardi.

It was a great journey, on the train through the Alps, through the Mont Blanc tunnels, right the way into Milan. And at Milan they met us with a bus and took us up into the mountains – off the train went the Italians, going home like they did (and still do) every August.

HARRY RADCLIFFE

Miners' Fortnight, that was a treat wasn't it? It meant we could go further afield – like up to Snowdon in North Wales. We'd go to the holiday camp in Pwllheli. That was marvellous entertainment. Those holiday camps were great with wonderful facilities.

That's where I learned to dance, at Butlin's Holiday Camp. I learned how to do it properly and then we danced, my wife and I, for years and years.

The holiday camps were very safe. You'd get one or two drunks but if they didn't behave, out they'd go. There was no messing about. No vandalism.

We'd take the full two weeks and go off to Rhyl first. We'd stay there for a week and then down through Betws y Coed to Pwllheli and the holiday camp.

Holiday camps gave people the chance to enjoy a relaxed but organised break.

MARCO CARINI

> In Italy, on holiday, we had a football team – just five-a-side – and we'd play the Italians in the farm field in the village. We never won many games, they were always too good for us.

JACK CARRADICE

> We always went to my parents' on holiday, each summer, first to Barnard Castle and then to Whickham when my father (he was a policeman) was posted there. After a small Welsh town, it was a real treat to see the big cities like Newcastle and Durham.

MARY PHILLIPS

> I loved Newcastle, all the shops and lights. It was so busy, so exciting. And then, sometimes, we'd go to places like Whitby and South Shields for the day, just for a change. We used to love going on the ferries across the River Tyne, seeing all the ships. It was quite exciting.

MAISIE WILLIAMS

> We always went on holiday in the country, often to the holiday camps – Butlin's and Warners. Then we went to Cornwall, to North Wales, all around. We had the same fortnight as the miners – you had to take your holidays then, otherwise you'd lose a week's wage if you went away.

In order to enjoy entertainment, like dancing, cinema or holidays, either with relatives or in places like a Butlin's Holiday Camp, women, in particular, needed to keep up with the fashions.

In the immediate post-war period, men tended to wear slacks and sports jacket. They were happy to be out of uniform and were not unduly concerned with fashion. The teddy boys with their Edwardian jackets and suede shoes came later, in the 1950s. For the moment there were more important things to spend money on than clothes.

Women, however, were determined to look their best. And the new world of post-war Britain demanded a new style of fashion.

SYLVIA BAILEY

> After the war the New Look came in – nipped-in waists and long skirts. And you always wore a hat. I remember I had this lovely black suit with a long skirt and this little black hat. I thought I looked wonderful.

Sylvia Bailey in the 'New Look' that was introduced after the war.

My mum was always interested in dressmaking. So even though it wasn't new material, she made the clothes for me. I remember her making a dress out of parachute silk and it turned out really nice.

Clothes rationing continued for several years after 1945 and, with material for dresses and skirts in short supply, women had to utilize the skills they had learned during the war.

DORIS CURTIS

Make do and mend, it was that sort of thing. You'd find old clothes and just turn them inside out. That's where your sewing came in – if you could sew you'd be all right. You'd pick things up, alter them and change them. I remember people even making coats out of blankets!

BARBARA JONES

The clothing coupons stopped just as I got married, I think. But up till then you'd try to make your own clothes. I remember that a lot of us made hats out of belts, coat belts. You brought them round from the back, crossed them over, brought them back and sewed them to the sides. It sort of stuck up a bit in the front – we thought they were very classy.

You'd eke out your clothes by borrowing from each other. I had three friends and we'd always swap and change our clothes. We were all about the same size – so we had four different dresses to choose from instead of one. If you owned a particular dress, well it was yours but very often you'd forgotten who'd owned it in the first place.

DILYS CHAPMAN

You couldn't just go out and buy your clothes. You were restricted to so many coupons and when they were gone that was it. For people interested in clothes – which all my sisters and I were – not to be able to go out and buy, like they do today, was hard. You'd think 'I really should have a winter coat!' But you just couldn't get it.

BARBARA JONES

Oh, Christian Dior's New Look – whereas the clothes were all on your knees during the war, now they were down to your ankles.

If you had a coat, you'd cut a straight line a few inches up from

The height of fashion – Barbara Jones.

the hem and then you'd put in a piece from some other old garment – say a blanket. And then you'd go up another six inches and put in another piece. It eked out what you had and it was still in fashion. I remember seeing a photograph of Princess Margaret at that time, dressed the same, just like that.

JOAN SMITH

What our mothers did was to add extra inches to the dresses to lengthen them – using a different colour sometimes. They also used to get old garments, perhaps from jumble sales, and rip them down, hang them in hanks and then wash them to straighten them. Then they'd rewind the wool.

Men used to have socks with pink feet and grey tops. Nobody minded, things were scarce. And at least they were warm!

EILUNED REES

Most of my clothes were hand-me-downs from my cousin. She was about fifteen years older then me but she was also a good needlewoman. So she'd make me things from her old clothes. We also had a good dressmaker in the village, Mrs Evans. She lived quite near, about two doors away. So if my mother could get hold of a remnant on the market she'd buy it and Mrs Evans would make suits and skirts from it. Or perhaps my cousin's coat would be made down into a skirt.

I didn't have many new clothes but after the war the New Look came in. It was a long time before it reached me but I can still remember my New Look coat – very unusual, a light-brown tweed one.

But no, we were quite thrilled with hand-me-downs. We didn't consider ourselves second-class citizens because we didn't know anything else. As long as we had something to wear! I was a tomboy anyway and it didn't matter very much.

JOAN SMITH

I was extremely small for my age, just like a couple of my family. And then we had the adolescent spurt. So when I left school at fourteen, I was four foot ten – but when I was sixteen, I was five foot four. It was a bit of a problem. I didn't get fatter but I got longer. I think I was the first person ever to wear a mini!

The late 1940s may well have been the years of austerity but there is no doubt that they opened up, possibly for the first time in history, leisure activities for all sections of society. Put simply, the working classes were finally given time to enjoy life. It was, in all respects, a truly remarkable period.

Chapter Six

Childhood Days

THE POST-WAR period brought both change and new experiences for many people – not least children. Having to adjust to the idea of a father who was actually there, a physical presence in the house rather than just a photograph on the sideboard, caused many children a great deal of heartache. And for some, whose fathers had died during the war, there was a further adjustment to be made.

SYLVIA BAILEY

I suppose I remember my stepfather more than my real dad. He was all right. I didn't particularly get on with him for several years. But then when he died, and he died quite early – my mum was widowed twice before she was fifty – I think I wept for him more than his own two children did. Because, later on, we got on really well.

Initially it wasn't easy. Well, you can imagine it. Ten years of being an only child, then a man suddenly comes onto the scene? It wasn't easy.

MILLIE JOHN

It was a bit strange at first when my husband came home from the war. We all had to get to know each other again. Ken – my son – and my husband, well it was strange for them. But Ken accepted him and they got on together. So it all worked out all right – it was just so wonderful, for us all to see him again.

For most children their only concern was doing what children do best – playing. And in a war-torn, cash-weak society, much of that playing involved dredging deeply on the imagination.

ROBERT NISBET

All of the children were playing at that time. I seem to remember the whole of my childhood, going on from three and four, right through to ten, twelve and so on, playing out in the woods and the fields in the way that children, perhaps, don't have the chance to do now.

Play was always important for youngsters – notice the matching jumpers (hand-knitted, undoubtedly) of the boys in this photograph and the sailor's hat, a souvenir from the war.

EILUNED REES

We weren't indoors very much in those days. We were playing on the beach, up in the castle or in the woods. In fact I spent more time in Wellington boots than I ever did in shoes. We were always out.

If we'd been to the pictures, and we'd seen, say *The Three Musketeers*, then we'd be acting it out for the rest of the week. Or *Robin Hood*, we'd be playing that. And *Sexton Blake*, of course, although that was a radio programme. We had to make our own entertainment and we were ingenious in our games.

JOAN SMITH

Our house on the Green in Pembroke was warm because we had thick walls and my mother always liked a good fire. The Meyricks, the local landowners, they'd chopped down their woods for the war effort but for a long while afterwards we'd go and collect these pieces of wood and big chunks that had been left lying about. We'd go up with a gambo and fill it up.

Joan Meyrick was about my age, and years later I got to know her quite well. When I told her about collecting the wood she said 'Oh I remember that.'

You see, they used to saddle up their horses and chase us out of the woods. Joan said 'You were always the Sheriff of Nottingham and we were Robin Hood.' And I smiled – 'Oh no,' I said. 'We were Robin Hood.' We laughed about that.

ROBERT NISBET

In the immediate post-war years there was very little option but to make your own fun. There were no football clubs or gym clubs. It was all very homespun.

One piece of entertainment I recall, not long after the war, was when a friend and I fell foul of another boy. And we decided to trap him and kill him. We decided to dig a large pit in a nearby field, put stakes at the bottom to impale him and cover it with reeds.

I think, in the end, this hole he was meant to fall into was about six inches by four inches. And the stakes to impale him were reeds that blew over immediately. The top level of grass just caved in. But, then, that was the sort of homespun entertainment we had at the time.

VALERIE CARINI

There was a river just by us and we used to go and play on the stones by that river. We were always having soakings, our socks were always getting wet. We were afraid of our

Marco Carini and his friends play happily in an old tent behind the family shop in Beaufort.

mothers giving us a row so we'd always be bashing them on the wall to get the water off – although I don't know what good we thought that would do!

We were always learning to ride bikes. My father had a bike, a ladies' bicycle, and we all used to try and ride on it. All the children would have a go. I had many a fall off that bike.

Inevitably, however, children had to grow up and distractions such as school began to intrude on the carefree days of playing and using your imagination.

ROBERT NISBET

I was almost a founder member of Fenton Infants' School. My first day in school would have been in 1946 but I remember an incident which must have taken place a little while before. My mother and I were walking past the Infants' School and a teacher came out, seemingly coincidentally, to the railings. She chatted with my mother and then said 'Would Robert like to come here one day?' And my mother said 'I'm sure he would.' It was only years later that I realised this was a put-up job, if ever there was one – being softened up to go to Infants School.

EILUNED REES

We had a very good school in Llansteffan. It was an old school, founded back in the nineteenth century – 1855, if my memory serves me correctly. The building had been condemned many times before the war but, despite the buildings, the education was wonderful. Very basic but wonderful.

I loved school and really wanted to go to University. I worked very hard for my eleven plus and I was very relieved that I'd passed.

ROBERT NISBET

I certainly remember the regime being a fairly strict one. The Headmistress was extremely strict in the way, perhaps, that Infants' School Headmistresses aren't anymore. I still have good memories of the school.

I remember on one occasion climbing the wall to look over into the boys' Primary School and suddenly seeing a whole new world, a new vista. It was one of those occasions in life when you look ahead to the future and are stunned and amazed.

I saw these boys running around in the field next door, playing football. I was amazed. And the sight of the road running away – I assumed it must be the road to London. In fact, as I realised later, it was the road to St David's.

EILUNED REES

Quite a few of us from the village went on to Carmarthen Grammar School (Boys' and Girls') but not many stayed on to do A Levels. Not many girls stayed on at all at this time but I was lucky. My father could see no reason at all why a girl shouldn't be educated. He said it gave her a choice in life.

That was different, even within my family. It wasn't that they were against my being educated but they really couldn't see the point of it. They'd say things like 'But suppose she gets married?' And my father would just say 'Well, at least she'll have the choice.' He was very much in favour of women being educated and liked the idea that you could have choice and control over what to do with your life.

ROBERT NISBET

In those days, in Primary School, we did quite an amount of local history and geography. When the MCC was touring Australia, we did all the Australian political geography and so on – because that's what the teacher was reading about in his newspaper in the evenings. We had quite a rounded education – I don't think the Eleven Plus pressure had started at that stage. In years to come, of course, it became more important and people focused more and more on the exam, on pass rates and so on.

Our teacher in the Primary School, Billy Childs, was a very enlightened teacher. He was one of the old-fashioned kind, in many ways, just a very, very good teacher.

As far as the teachers themselves were concerned the post-war period was an exciting time. The new tripartite system had just come into existence and there was a mood of optimism in the air.

JACK CARRADICE

We felt we were on the threshold of great things. For the first time there was a proper system of education in this country, with children being provided with a choice of subjects and style of learning that best suited them. Of course, ultimately, it didn't work out quite like that. But then, in the late forties, we felt like we were at the cutting edge of real change. That's not to say it was easy work – there was a lot of overcrowding in those days.

GLYN MILLER

I had over 60 children in my first class, ages ranging from seven to nearly twelve. I don't remember any discipline problems but it certainly wasn't easy.

My first school in Wales was an old industrial school, Bryndu Colliery School. About half the pupils came from the old RAF station at Stormy Down which was occupied by squatters – quite official, I believe, as they paid rent to the Local Authority. Over half the children came from these squatters on Stormy Down.

They were bussed across to Bryndu every day. At that time the Local Authority was building a new estate at North Cornelly and when it was ready all the squatters went to live there – which meant our pupil number went down by over half, overnight!

Despite the new Tripartite System, school was still largely a matter of learning by rote, often in classrooms totally unsuited for the task.

One memory that stays with many people is the drive to help people save money. Every Monday morning the strange ritual of Savings Stamps – National Savings as it was known – was acted out in schools up and down the country. It was a sensible and well-intentioned scheme but as VALERIE CARINI remembers, it was not always as effective as the organisers hoped.

VALERIE CARINI

Every Monday, you used to take in your sixpence and in return you got a stamp. When you'd filled up the book, some people would buy a certificate and save up even more. But we couldn't manage that. We'd wait until Christmas, then we'd take it all out and buy presents for every member of the family.

Lots of children saved. I think most of them took out a savings stamp each Monday. I remember the Secretary coming round and collecting the money. We'd all have this special card to take home. It was a good way of saving but, as I say, we never managed to get beyond Christmas.

National Savings.

Christmas was perhaps the most important of all festivities as far as children were concerned. Once summer was over, everyone began longing for December 25th – and in those days of austerity, the great day really did mean something very special.

VALERIE CARINI

> Christmas was very important to us. We'd all be waiting, looking everywhere to see where mother had hidden things – you know, in the wardrobes, everywhere.
>
> There were three of us, three sisters, and my aunt had a shop in Beaufort. She used to buy three of everything for Christmas. If we had sweets or fruit we'd ask 'Have you eaten yours yet?' We wouldn't eat ours until the others had finished.
>
> Maybe, sometimes, my aunt couldn't get three things exactly the same. Then we were always a bit despondent because we didn't have exactly the same as the others.

MYRTLE JENKINS

> After the war I worked in a shop, doing the alterations. I also worked in the Leather Store in Aberdare – I was there for twelve years in all. It was hard work but it was fun as well, especially at Christmas time. Oh it was lovely then!
>
> People used to come in – they'd been saving through the year for different toys. And they'd come in at Christmas time to pick up their toys. Everything had a number on it and, of course, there were three floors so you didn't know which floor the present was stored on.

VALERIE CARINI

> We'd take, literally, hours wandering around Boots or Woolworths, just wondering what we were going to buy. It was mostly Woolworths, you know, with all the sixpenny things they had there.
>
> We'd buy everyone a present. My father would, maybe, have a tin of brilliantine for his hair. But everyone had something.

MYRTLE JENKINS

> You'd see the parents coming into the shop – 'Don't show it now,' they'd whisper. 'Pack it underneath the counter.' Oh, it was a fun shop at Christmas time; it was lovely!

MAISIE WILLIAMS

> There wasn't a lot of money but the children never went without. If anyone was going to do without it would be me.
>
> Toys? Well, you used to make a lot. Yes, the men would make a lot of wooden toys. It wasn't like it is now – they've got too much these days.

For many children, the seasons gave purpose to their year. Events and festivals like the Sunday-school Whitsun treat, Easter or Christmas were important.

Christmas, every child's dream – a selection of 1940s Christmas Cards.

SYLVIA BAILEY

We didn't have many trips or holidays at that time. Usually it was just Barry Island, once a year. That and the Whitsun treat which was usually linked with the churches.

Gabalfa Baptist Chapel used to have an Annual Treat – I think that's what it was called. We'd go out to St Mellons and often, now, I drive past and think 'Oh yes, we used to come here for the Whitsun treat.'

EILUNED REES

The church and chapel were always well supported in the village. Remember, all the villages had their own vicars at that time. In Llansteffan there was a Baptist Minister and a Methodist Minister as well.

Even if you couldn't afford a holiday there were still day trips to the seaside to look forward to, often organised by the churches and chapels. And when you were at the seaside you almost always saw a Punch and Judy show.

There was such a lot going on. It wasn't just chapel on a Sunday, either. There was a Band of Hope for the children, prayer meetings for the adults. There were parties, Christmas parties and things like that.

And, of course, there was the Gymanfa Ganu, where everybody joined in. There were always rehearsals for them. They played a very important part in people's lives. The church and chapel were the centre of social life in the village then.

As children grew up, however, two important events began to impinge themselves on their lives – work and friends of the opposite sex.

JOAN SMITH

I left school at fourteen and went up to Lancashire to work in my uncle's cotton mill. I was there for about eighteen months and then my father came to fetch me home.

SYLVIA BAILEY

I left school, believe it or not, when I was just thirteen. When my children hear that they say 'You couldn't have left school at thirteen.' But I did.

I went to a Commercial College – Frederick Street Commercial College. And you could do that. As long as you took English and Maths, it was classed as Continuing Education. Because my father had been killed during the war, it was all paid for by the War Services or some sort of body like that. They paid the fees for me to go to this Commercial College. It was the making of me, really.

JOAN SMITH

When I came back to Pembroke, I didn't work for a while. Then it was early spring. My father used to rent three fields up Golden Hill. This girl and I went up to feed the chickens one morning and found they were planting potatoes on Bush Hill.

We went over to see and they offered us a job. We didn't get home till after dinnertime. The man said we were good workers – he called for us next day and so we went down to Stackpole and worked the entire summer there.

SYLVIA BAILEY

At the Commercial College I learned shorthand and typing and bookkeeping – but I never learned much English and Maths there. That was a bit of a farce really.

JOAN SMITH

There used to be what, today, you would call a Monkey Walk. There wasn't a lot to do in the town so the young boys and girls would walk from one end of the place to the other every Sunday night. They'd be hoping to meet up with whoever they fancied at the time.

SYLVIA BAILEY

I was a bit wayward, to say the least, when I was younger – I'm not sorry to admit it. I came home from Commercial College one day and my mother said to me 'Where were you yesterday?' I said 'College. And then I went to the pictures.' 'Yes,' she said. 'I know you went to the pictures.' And then she threw the newspaper at me.

And there was me, on the front page of *The Echo* – with Donald Houston and Jean Simmons! They'd just made a film, *The Blue Lagoon*. And the headline read 'Teenagers Waiting for Stars at Cardiff Station'. I nearly got expelled from the College for that!

JOAN SMITH

Pembroke was a garrison town – and there was an aerodrome at Carew, not far away. And the dockyard at Pembroke Dock always had plenty of sailors. So men were never in short supply.

So the local boys really had to compete with this. I wasn't in Pembroke when the Yanks came but apparently they had a really good time.

The growth from childhood to adulthood has never been easy and adolescent reactions in the post-war years were no different from what they had been before or after. Yet in the late 1940s, young people could look ahead with optimism and hope – whatever things were like now they could only get better in the years ahead.

Chapter Seven

Grudge and Grind

AN EVENT like the Second World War was bound to create tension and bitterness. In a global conflict where death, destruction and terror had been brought closer to the civilian population of Britain than ever before, such feelings were intense.

Different people reacted to their emotions in different ways, particularly once the war was over and they had time to sit and consider all that had gone on over the previous six years. For some the bitterness would never go away. Others were able to come to terms with their feeling and consign the events of the war to history. For some there was a degree of compromise.

JACK CARRADICE

I can't say I hated the Japanese or the Germans. Of course I hated what they'd done: the German concentration camps, the Japanese prisoner-of-war camps. We fought them and they were good soldiers, make no mistake about that – the atrocities were something else, really. I can't say they're my favourite people, either nation, but I don't really hate them.

The return of a soldier from a Japanese prisoner-of-war camp.

GLYN MILLER

I do not like the Japanese people. I don't know if I should be saying this but they haven't properly apologised for the foul things their army did during the war. For example, when they took Rangoon they bayoneted all the patients in the hospital beds. And what they did to the nurses . . . So no, I don't like them particularly.

DAVID JENKINS

When the Regiment came back, before I was demobbed, we were posted down to Neath. We were looking after German prisoners of war.

One of them – I used to say to my wife – you should have heard him play the piano. They're nice people, the Germans, nice people. They've got it all up top. And this fellow was playing the piano. Oh he was wonderful, wonderful.

VERA JAMESON had been evacuated to Wales from East Ham, during the early part of the war. When German bombers dropped high explosives onto Cwmparc in the Rhondda on 29th April, 1941, twenty-seven people were killed. Among the dead were Vera Jameson's sister and two brothers.

VERA JAMESON

I was evacuated to Felixstowe and from there we went to the Rhondda. I was lucky enough to be evacuated to a mother with a daughter and a grandfather. They were very nice people.

The bombing of Cwmparc was a traumatic event for the village and for people like Vera Jameson in particular. Buried for ten hours in the rubble of her bombed house, she was hospitalised for a long time.

VERA JAMESON

When my mother and father came to see me, they kept telling me the children had been evacuated. I knew my sister was dead but they kept saying that Joan, George and Arthur were evacuated. I was never told that my brothers and sisters were actually dead.

When we came home from the evacuation, there used to be two pewter art pots on the mantelpiece. One held a gun and the other three bullets. They were there for when my dad went to Germany. He said he was going to shoot three children.

Now, my dad couldn't kill a chicken! After the war there was an amnesty but he still wouldn't get rid of the gun and bullets. So one day I just took them. It was November and there was a good thick fog. I was fourteen by then and walking to work. I just took the gun and bullets and dropped them in the road. As far as I'm concerned they're still there.

Dad's idea was revenge. I didn't think like that. In the early 1960s, I went on holiday to Austria. Dad was really annoyed that I'd gone anywhere near

Germany. While I was there, this German came up to me – I was fat then and he said he liked his women fat. I said I liked my brothers alive and pushed him away. But that was all, that's how I dealt with it.

The Atom Bomb, and the effect it had on Hiroshima and Nagasaki, dominated the thinking of many people in these post-war years. It was the ultimate terror weapon, taking up where Hitler's V1 and V2 rockets had left off. With the Cold War battle-lines firmly and clearly drawn, nobody even wanted to imagine what a war involving weapons of mass destruction would be like.

In his book *A Cardiff Family in the Forties*, Malcolm Pill has described his father's reaction on hearing about the atom bomb attack on Japan. It was not quite what the youngster had expected.

MALCOLM PILL

I was surprised at his gloomy reaction. Of course he was pleased that the war would be over sooner and a lot of men like him would not be killed but he quietly explained to me the consequences of living in a world with this terrible weapon.

JACK CARRADICE

We were horrified by what it had done, the Atom Bomb – and the thought of what might happen if anyone should drop one on us. Everyone said it would come from the Russians – personally I was always more worried about the Yanks!

As the years went on, however, it was only the threat of one big bang that kept the great powers away from each other's throats. At least, that's what I believe. There's certainly an argument that it was a lot safer world after the Atom Bomb was invented.

Fear of the Atom Bomb and what it might do was only one element in a mood of resignation that many people felt at that time. It was a mood that crept in gradually, after the euphoria of Labour's election victory had begun to wear off – once people realised that the new Socialist government was fighting (and possibly losing) a difficult battle to make Britain economically viable once more.

There were plenty of jobs in post-war Wales but the wages remained relatively low. Luxury goods were in short supply and even the staple ingredients like sugar remained rare. When people stared at the bombsites that littered and scarred the cities and towns for many years after the war, it was hard not to agree with the sceptics who asked 'Who won this damned war?'

People in the street of almost any town at this time looked pale and drawn, their clothes threadbare or recycled, which was ironic because, owing to the balanced diet that had been forced upon people by rationing, the population of the country was probably better nourished and better fed than it had ever been before. What really summed up the mood of the people, however, was the amazing propensity of the British to queue. And Wales and the Welsh were no different.

Not an unhappy face anywhere in the queue. World War II and the days of austerity that followed it taught people how to queue for the necessities in life.

EILUNED REES

My aunt, who lived near Llanelli, would join any queue. It didn't matter what it was, if there was a queue she would join it. When she died, at the age of 90, my cousin found tins of salmon in her wardrobe, dating back to the war and just afterwards. She'd stockpiled them through joining queues.

BARBARA JONES

There was always a queue in those days. That's one thing that came out of the war, it made people queue. Before the war there'd be a crowd of people all pushing and shoving for the bus or tram and the strongest got on first. The weaker ones were left for the next bus.

But with rationing – and, remember, that went on after the war – you just had to queue. It reached into other areas as well. You didn't all stand in a crowd and shove when a bus came. You stood in an orderly queue. So I suppose some good came out of the war.

EILUNED REES

Queues were part of our lives, even after the war. There was such a terrible shortage of things. The word would get around that, say, a shop in Carmarthen had a stock of shoes. The word would be round like wildfire and then there'd be a rush to queue outside the shop. It was amazing.

Queuing certainly seemed to be something of a national pastime. Queuing for food, for entry to the cinema, for the bus or railway train, perhaps reflected the discipline that had been instilled into people during the war years. That discipline was also turned to other areas of life – like finding a job after demobilisation.

LESLIE GRIFFITHS

I was in the Royal Welch Fusiliers during the war. You had good mates there and got on with everybody. The Royal Welch Fusiliers had a big black flash on the back of their uniform and I was very proud of that.

But coming back after the war, what you really felt was relief. I was very excited because I came back to my own trade, building. We were repairing all the bombed-out buildings. All my life I spent building.

EILUNED REES

There were two factories in Carmarthen, two milk factories and quite a few women worked there. We also had quite a few men employed on the farms around the village at this time.

BARBARA JONES

I was home about a month after being demobbed and I was getting a bit fed up then because most of my friends were working. So I got a job at Sherman's, the Pools' place. I went there in the claims' department. I liked it until the January of 1947 when we had an awful lot of snow all over the country. Most of the football matches were cancelled, for four, five, six weeks afterwards. So we were just sat in the office – we must have had the tidiest cupboards in Cardiff! I looked around and got another job – Bonus Clerk in a factory.

Barbara Jones, not long after she had been demobbed and begun work in Cardiff.

ROY CHAPMAN

After demob, I came back to Cardiff to work in British Telecommunications. I'd started with them as a Youth in Training, as it was known. They kept my job open while I was away in the RAF and when I came back I took on Docks Maintenance in the docks area, as it was in those days.

I was a skilled workman, a maintenance engineer, repairing the telephones. Eventually I became an assistant engineer, quite different from what I'd been doing in the RAF, and then Transport Officer looking after about 1200 vehicles.

DENIS MORGAN

After the war I became Estates and Way Leaves Officer for the South Wales Electricity Board. If, say, you wanted to build an electricity line between Cardiff and Brecon, I was responsible for getting permission from the owners or occupiers of the land. And for getting planning permission for the lines.

Finally, when the lines were erected, I had to go around and see everybody and agree compensation for the damage we'd done. It was a bit complicated at times.

DAVID JENKINS

We got demobbed up near Peterborough. We were allowed to keep our uniform coat – and that used to go on the bed when I came home. Anyway I soon said 'I want to go back to work.' My wife, Myrtle, she said 'But you haven't been home a week yet!' A month off, that was compulsory, you had to stay home a month.

Anyway, after that I went back to the Red and White bus company. I started work again in 1947 and worked there until 1951 when I went to the Wales Gas Board as a fitter.

MAISIE WILLIAMS

After I came back to Wales, I used to see the Glascoed bus going past the door and I said to myself 'I'll be on that bus one day.' So I applied. My husband was a miner. He met me in town afterwards and my sister-in-law said 'Where have you been, all dressed up?' And I said 'I've been for an interview.' My husband looked. 'What for?' he said. 'For work,' I said

Well, when we got home he asked me all about it. He was annoyed, he wouldn't talk to me for a month. He was a good husband, very good, but he was a jealous man.

'Well,' he said, 'don't I bring in enough?' And we talked and I said 'If I can earn a little bit we can go places and get more things.' He thought it over and after a month or so he was setting the alarm to make sure I'd be up ready to go off to work.

For the Italian families of Wales, release from the internment was exactly like coming home from the forces. They had to pick up the pieces and begin business once more – in many cases almost from scratch.

PETER SIDOLI

It wasn't easy after the war. Rationing was still in force and even things like hay for the horses – for the ice cream round – was on ration. So we couldn't even get a horse – we had to hire one to start with. The horse we had later he knew the route better than we did – you could have been asleep and he'd still go round the streets.

MARCO CARINI

The shop in Beaufort had carried on all through the war. Tony left school and went into the business, then Joe – he had a bit of a farm but he helped in the shop, too. I was in there from the age of nine, always in there serving after school.

Tony expanded the shop, selling a lot of different things because the cafés were starting to go down a bit. My mother died in the business and when my father retired, Tony and Joe took it over.

I used to help them by relieving them, perhaps giving them a week's holiday, or going in on a Sunday so they could have time off. Or maybe on a Wednesday evening.

Helping to get the economy going by working – in whatever type or style of job that best suited you – was considered essential and men and women dutifully trudged off to work each morning, conscious that they were helping to put Britain back on her feet.

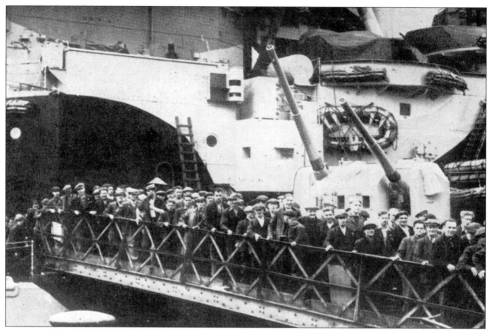

Getting the country back to work. Shipbuilders stream home across the gangplank at the end of the day.

Sometimes the process of actually getting to work was far from easy.

MAISIE WILLIAMS

There were only a few cars about in those days – so you were fortunate if you had a lift. We usually went by bus or just walked. Oh, we did a lot of walking in those days – even for your courting you went walking. Nowadays you just jump into the car, you can't walk from here to there. But not then.

VALERIE CARINI

There were no cars around in those days. So if we wanted to go anywhere we went on the bus or on the train. My two sisters and me, we went to Bristol on holiday but we went by train. People just wouldn't do it these days.

BARBARA JONES

You had to queue for any form of public transport. To be honest, that's where I really missed the uniform. You see, if you were in uniform, you only had to stand at a bus stop and somebody would pull up and give you a lift. And you took the lift in those days. Today you're frightened to death but back then everybody was very nice to you – especially if you were in uniform!

EILUNED REES

I had a second-hand bike – in fact it was third hand. I adored my bike and went all over the place on it. The only people who had cars in those days were people like Dai Carrier with his taxis, ministers of religion and the gentleman farmers of the area.

We knew every car in the village by its sound. There were so few cars around that if we heard a car coming down the narrow lane, we'd push our bikes into the hedge and say 'That's so and so'.

Finding suitable transport for courting was not easy in these post-war years, as Bill Williams recalls. He was serving as a Regular in the RAF at the time, based at Llandow in the Vale of Glamorgan.

BILL WILLIAMS

I used to go into Bridgend and there I met this little nurse. Eventually I married her, but before that I used to go on the little railway that ran to Bridgend through Llantwit Major. But the train back used to leave at about quarter past ten and the cinema didn't let out until ten. That didn't leave much time to say goodnight to the nurse.

So I decided to take my bike. I'd cycle to Bridgend, leave the bike at the Left Luggage in the station and go to the pictures. After a goodnight session with my nurse, I'd cycle back to camp. I always remember it was very lonely on that bike-ride. There weren't many cars on the road in those days. One place I didn't like going past was Dunraven. There was a lodge there and it was always a bit eerie when you cycled past there.

The other real scare I got was one foggy night as I was coming into Wick. I was cycling along and, suddenly, there was a big white shape going across the road. I thought 'Oh my God, what's that?' When I went past, I realised it was a big white horse that had escaped from a field.

I reckon it must have been love that made me do it. And I must have been pretty fit, too.

Some people were lucky and did have the use of a car, usually because it was part of the man's business or because it was a hobby.

All that's best in Britain..

Year in, year out, from Cornwall to the lonely islands of the Hebrides, Britain's fishermen fight the unending battle of the sea to reap its harvest . . . . . with each encounter gleaning new knowledge and experience . . . . . . in the same way the accumulated skill and experience of generations of engineers go into the products of the Standard Motor Company, representing as they do in every detail of their design ' all that's best in Britain.'

The Standard Vanguard

Manufactured by
THE STANDARD MOTOR CO. LTD., COVENTRY
London : 27, Davies Street, Grosvenor Square, W.1.
Telephone : MAYfair 9111

In the first few years of peace very few people owned motor cars but, gradually, more and more families began to see the advantages of having their own transport. This advertising poster from the period links car ownership with the British love of, and reliance upon, the sea.

DENIS MORGAN

Because I was working for the South Wales Electricity Board, I had to have transport. I had a van first, then a bit later on, a car. I had that all the time I was working for them. All my running costs were paid for by the Board – along with the mileage.

GLYN MILLER

I suppose I've had a dozen cars over the years. The first was a Reliant Regal Mark VI – three wheels!

The roads weren't much good for motoring then, mind you. I remember going by car to Birmingham and it took five hours to drive there – no motorways, just the roads across the Malverns.

DORIS CURTIS

We always had cars. They were Leslie's passion. He was an auto electrician and he was always buying a car, doing it up, then selling it and buying another. He never made any money at it – everything went back into buying the next car.

We had all sorts of cars: Morris and Rover, Austins, even an Alvis once. Mostly we had Vauxhalls because that's

Doris Curtis behind the wheel of one of the family cars. She had learned to drive in the Land Army.

the firm Leslie trained with. He was always working on his cars. In those days you charged your own batteries, did everything yourself. I remember helping him to strip down dynamos and washing them out with petrol. I don't think I can remember a time when we weren't buying a car of one sort or another.

For young men the lure of motorbikes was particularly strong. Many of them had driven bikes during their war service; for others – just reaching the age when motorbikes and cars were becoming interesting – they reflected a desire for freedom and independence. HARRY HIGHMAN had worked in the Naval Propellant Factory at Caerwent during the war and was interested in all things mechanical.

HARRY HIGHMAN

When the war ended in 1945, petrol was more easily available and, like most eighteen-year-olds, I wanted to get a motorbike. In those days, however, they were almost unobtainable, unless you could get hold of one of the ex-army bikes that the government was selling off as war surplus. That's what I was looking at but then a fellow worker at RNPF Caerwent told me he had a very old, broken-down motorbike lying in his coal house. I could have it for free if I wanted.

Naturally enough, Harry Highman accepted his friend's offer. After unearthing the bike from beneath what seemed like several tons of coal, he was able to study his new possession.

HARRY HIGHMAN

The engine was dismantled because of a broken piston, the tyres were deflated and my mate told me that the bike hadn't been on the road since 1922. It was a 1919 Levi's bike with a two-stroke engine. It had extremely wide handlebars and a long, square-section petrol tank. Amazingly, when we pumped up the tyres they stayed inflated. But how could I get it home? The only solution was to wheel it all the way, a distance of nearly twelve miles. And when I got home my parents were not very pleased with my new acquisition. They considered it a very dangerous, unsafe means of transport.

Harry Highman spent many hours fixing up his bike. The noise from the engine, not to mention the smoke from the exhaust, was awful. The bike was not taxed or insured so his jaunts were confined to quick trips up and down the road. Then he was informed that the local policeman had been making enquiries about a very noisy motorbike that had been seen and heard running around the area.

HARRY HIGHMAN

My parents told me to get rid of the bike. Well, I was eighteen years old and you just did as you were told in those days. What I did – and, later, I really regretted my action because, remember, this was already a vintage bike that would now be worth many thousands of pounds – was to saw up the frame and wheels and bury them in our allotment. Today that allotment lies under the M4 motorway. I kept the engine with the intention of using it as the drive for a lathe I was making at work. It was a job I didn't complete and eventually I just gave the engine to a colleague.

It was to be several years before Harry Highman, like many other young men, moved on to his next vehicle – and then it was to be, not a motorbike, but a car. Money was a constant problem and worry for most people in these post-war days and the simple act of earning enough to put food on the table was uppermost in the minds of most families. Thankfully it was a situation that did not last.

As the Forties began to run out into the more affluent Fifties, the situation became easier. People gradually became more property-conscious, more acquisitive. Whereas in the years immediately after the war, the purchase of a house was beyond most people, by 1948-49 it had fallen within the remit of many.

There was very little unemployment in the post-war years, despite the fact that many of those opposed to the Welfare State thought it would create a nation of 'shirkers' who had no desire to work and every desire to receive free handouts.

GLYN MILLER

> When I started teaching, I found it very difficult. On £360 a year, I wasn't earning enough for the Building Societies to give me a mortgage. So we rented accommodation. As the years went on, I did get increments on my salary, probably £12 or £15 a year. It was a big thing, then.

DORIS CURTIS

> We didn't have a house of our own. We lived with my in-laws until Tony, my son, was almost twelve. And then we came to Leslie's aunt's place in Kilgetty. She left us her house when she died and we went to live there. It was our first real home together.

DENIS MORGAN

> To be honest I didn't find it so hard to buy a house after the war. My wife and I happened to be passing this house one day, in the car, and there was a notice saying 'For Sale'. We went in and had a look – quite out of my class, of course. It had six bedrooms and two acres of land.
>
> But it was owned by the Coal Board and I rang up the Estates Manager. I didn't know the price, even. He said '£4,000'. I just said 'Oh I can't give you that. I'll give you three and a half.' Just like that, off the cuff, no mortgage, nothing.
>
> 'Righto,' he said. 'I'll consider it.' Two days later I got a letter saying that I could have the house for three and a half thousand pounds. It needed an awful lot of work, mind, as it had been neglected. But it was mine.

Chapter Eight

And So it Goes On

IT WAS a reasonable expectation to believe things might be different in the post-war years. After all, people had put up with considerable hardship in order to win the war and while nobody expected a paradise to arise overnight, the austerity years of 1945 to 1950 caught many by surprise.

Food was actually scarcer in Britain after 1945 than it had been during the war. America had curtailed its lend-lease programme soon after the end of hostilities and, with Britain almost bankrupt, there was little money with which to buy essential food supplies. As a consequence, items such as sugar, tea, butter, eggs and cheese continued to be rationed until 1952. Bacon and meat were actually kept 'on the ration' for a further two years.

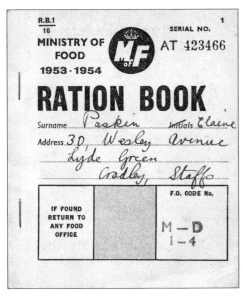 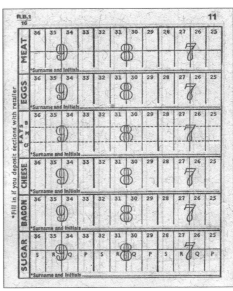

Rationing continued until the early 1950s, a hard burden for people who had suffered for so long during the war.

JOAN SMITH

Rationing carried on for quite a while after the war. I don't know exactly when it finished but I remember the worst thing of all was the shortage of sugar. We all loved sugar in our family and when we fetched the rations once a week, well, to have a cup of tea with sugar? It was wonderful.

I remember putting Golden Syrup in my tea. It was horrible, it turned the tea black. But it was better than tea on its own.

RON SUMPTION

Austerity? You just had to get used to it. It was the norm in those days and you accepted it. I think back then we were resilient enough to keep going. That was the key.

ROBERT NISBET

I think, as a small boy, it was the sweet-rationing that affected me most. I do remember all the books of coupons, for all sorts of goods, butter amongst them. But the thing that really bit into my soul was the lack of sweets.

Sweet-rationing affected all sections of society, not just the children. And sometimes people found ingenious ways of getting around the problem.

HARRY RADCLIFFE

I chewed PKs when I was working in the mine. I always had this PK in my mouth, PK chewing gum. Then the management of the colliery and a few staff got together and formed a little canteen. There was one chap there, he liked cheese – and I liked these PKs. So I'd swop my cheese ration for his PKs – all done on mutual agreement.

MAISIE WILLIAMS

Everybody was friendly with each other at that time. If you had something you didn't like, you just exchanged it with somebody else.

We also used to buy sheets of clothing coupons off men who were leaving Glascoed, men who were going into the forces perhaps – on 'Call Up' or because they could earn better money there. They'd sell children's clothing coupons for a pound – sometimes you were lucky and got them for ten shillings but usually it was a pound.

Owning a sweet shop sometimes presented young children like Marco Carini with a temptation that was very hard to resist.

MARCO CARINI

People wanted their coupons for food. So their sweet ration was a bit of a problem. We used to have the caramels, the sweets, in a big sack, a one-cwt sack, at the bottom of our stairs. And as kids, we'd be pinching the sweets out of the jar. Terrible, really, but that's how it was in those days.

Bureaucracy, of course, affected the shop owners as well.

MARCO CARINI

We were allowed to buy sweets through the trade. We had forms to fill in and you'd be allowed so many coupons for so many sweets. My brother used to be counting these coupons every three months to take them into the food centre in Ebbw Vale. Talk about the Gestapo, the people in there were terrible. If you were four or five coupons short it was a case of 'You can't have this next time' or 'You can't have that.' They were really nasty to him

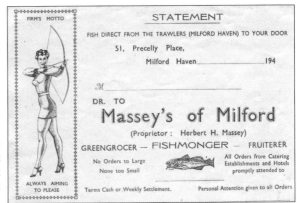

Fish, surprisingly enough, was often in short supply in the post-war years – but you would never think so to look at this elegantly designed invoice from Massey's of Milford.

People adapted to the shortages, however, making the best they could out of difficult situations.

JOAN SMITH

I don't remember what the actual meat ration was after the war but, to be honest, it didn't worry us very much. We knew a lot of farmers and so we always had rabbits and plenty of vegetables. I never went hungry, I must say that. My mother was a very good cook and if we went short of anything it was clothes – not food.

EILUNED REES

Although food rationing went on until just before I went to University, we didn't do too badly down here because my father had a garden and we also had a plot.

My father, who was a policeman, used to help the farmers. He couldn't get paid but he'd have a row of beans in one field, potatoes in another. We didn't have any luxuries, just basic food really.

We had pigs as well. My father rented a pigsty. If you reared a pig, half went to the Ministry of Food but you could keep the other half. So we didn't starve. We didn't have many sweet things but it didn't seem to matter because we'd never had them. We just didn't know anything else.

ROBERT NISBET'S father was a vet in Pembrokeshire. In those post-war days veterinary work was concerned, predominantly, with the agricultural side of things as the days of 'pampered pets' did not arrive until very much later.

ROBERT NISBET

> I remember my father coming home with a turnip sticking out of his jacket pocket. It probably helped – a curious little black economy
>
> There was one occasion when he diagnosed some valuable beast which had severe pains as having a nail in her stomach. He got it out after an operation – it was in the days when vets, like GPs, did their own surgery. Anyway he produced the nail and it was placed in a glass case in the local pub, a position of honour. I think my father got all the turnips he wanted for ever more.

Gradually, however, as the years went on conditions in Wales (and the rest of Britain) began to improve. Standards of living rose, food imports increased and by the end of the1940s, people were at last able to enjoy the results of their labours.

RON SUMPTION

> I can remember when a lot of sweets suddenly came into the shops. It was wonderful. But more than that I remember bananas. My sister worked for a greengrocer, a wholesale greengrocer, and during the school holidays, I used to help out on the lorries.
>
> I can remember when bananas came back, I ate so many of them I never wanted to see another banana in my life. Absolutely true – I can remember that.

MARCO CARINI

> Things got better as the years went on. The cigarette trade built up and the café too. Yes, it definitely got better.

Many improvements in society had been delayed by the war but as the effects of the conflict receded people gradually began to see some of the benefits of modern technology.

EILUNED REES

> There was no electricity in our village until 1952, apart from in a few select places. No, we lived with candles, oil lamps and Aladdin Lamps, which were superior to the others. All the shops sold paraffin for the lamps – and candles, of course.
>
> We used to go and visit family in Llangennech and the first thing we'd do was put the light switch on. You didn't realise how wonderful it was, electricity.

It wasn't just electricity that arrived in most places after the war. Llansteffan – like most remote villages – had other needs, too.

EILNUED REES

> We had a no running water in those years. It was just the old earth closet at the top of the garden until the water closets came in 1953.

Everything had been delayed because of the war. Our school had been condemned years before but we didn't get a new one until 1953. I think there would have been more car ownership, too, if there hadn't been a war. But, with petrol rationing and most of the men away in the forces, car ownership was delayed for quite a while.

For most people the post-war years meant simply getting on with life. They did it to the best of their ability and, if they were lucky, were able to enjoy some little leisure activity as well. For some people, however, getting on with life meant carrying on where the wartime servicemen had left off.

BILL WILLIAMS was a Regular in the RAF during the war and when peace came in 1945 he was faced with a situation where many of his comrades were discharged and sent home. He, on the other hand, had to remain in the service.

BILL WILLIAMS

I was an aircraft apprentice. I'd joined in January 1937 and would have finished my course at Christmas 1939. But the war broke out in September and we were pushed out early. I always like to think that a fortnight after the war started Hitler's fate was decided because I passed out of RAF Halton!

At the end of the war I was lucky because I was sent on a course. I was an air-frame fitter and they sent us on a conversion course – all the engine fitters did the air-frame course and we did the engine fitters course. It was a year's course so, for the year after the war – when the air force was disintegrating almost – we were sort of sheltered because we were on the course.

It was a bit unsettling, I suppose, because there was such a lot of disorganisation. As I say, the Air Force was disintegrating, their reason for existence was gone. But I suppose I missed a lot of it because of this course.

I wasn't too worried about everyone going home because, as an apprentice, you sign on for twelve years. It was my career – that was just the way it was. It was life.

Sometimes continuing to serve your country meant leaving Wales, as policemen HEDLEY ONIONS and JOHN GODFREY recall.

HEDLEY ONIONS

At this time the Government, via the Foreign Office, had been approached to start a police and prisons' mission for the retraining and supervision of the Royal Greek Gendarmerie. They'd been disbanded by the occupation forces of Italy and Germany during the war.

So I was sent out to Athens. My wife came out to join me and in 1947 the Dodecanese islands were given back to Greece as reparations for the war. I was appointed to take over the islands and so my wife and I moved there on a Greek landing ship, complete with all the Gendarmerie personnel. I was centred on the island of Kos.

After the war, Hedley Onions had been sent to help retrain the Greek police force. This photograph shows him (centre) with a member of his staff and his Greek interpreter, just before he returned to Wales.

JOHN GODFREY

I went into the army just after the war. Because I'd been a police cadet, I went into the Military Police, SID, Special Branch.

While I was in Berlin I had a call, one morning, to go to Spandau Prison. At that time there were between nine and eleven prisoners there. They were looked after, month by month – one month by the English, the next by the American, then the Russians, then the French.

On this particular occasion the Americans were in charge and it was reported that an American had been assaulted by a British soldier – that meant it was our investigation. I interviewed this American who told me he'd gone to a pub in Spandau village and had been assaulted by a soldier wearing a skirt – the assailant was a member of the Black Watch who were stationed there, about 1500 of them.

I said 'If it's any good I'll have an ID parade. We'll see if you can pick out the man from the Black Watch – all 1500 of them!' No chance.

HEDLEY ONIONS

When I arrived in Greece I was completely green with no knowledge of the Greek language. So I was equipped with a Greek interpreter. We became quite close and, on our travels, I tried to learn a little Greek. So perhaps I'd order our meal in a tavern in my pidgin Greek.

My interpreter, who was very jealous of the purity of his language, his ancient language, became frustrated on one occasion. And he said to me 'You know, sir, you're speaking Greek like a native.' 'Really?' I said. 'Yes,' he said, 'like an African native!' That certainly put me in my place.

Hedley Onions at work in his office in Greece.

JOHN GODFREY

While I was visiting Spandau, the officer said 'You must have a look around.' He took me, then, to this cell. Hess was in there and all he was doing, the only job he had, was making envelopes in his cell. He had paper and gum. He'd cut the paper to size and make the envelopes.

I wasn't allowed to speak to him but it was undoubtedly the same man I'd seen earlier on during the war when I was a police cadet in Wales. We'd been taken to White Castle near Abergavenny and while we were there two army vehicles came and out came this stocky fella. 'That's Hess,' our sergeant said, 'he's in a local hospital nearby.'

And the man in the cell at Spandau was the same man, Rudolph Hess.

For people like BILL WILLIAMS, who later settled in Wales, the post-war period saw their first contact with the country. And often they were astounded by what they saw.

BILL WILLIAMS

After the war, I was posted to a mobile repair unit at Shrewsbury and, as Wales was the area we covered, I once had to go across the country, across central Wales, to Aberporth, by train – plus my bike. I must have changed trains four times and every time there was another train waiting in the station. The first weekend I was there I was riding around, looking at the coast. I'd never seen anything so beautiful as the Welsh coastline around Aberporth.

On this mobile unit I did a lot of time at various Welsh stations. I went to Pembrey, near Llanelli, and on the train going down all our chaps were talking about a place called Slash. I didn't know what they were on about but it turned out it was the RAF name for Llanelli!

The post-war years saw the dismantling and destruction of thousands of weapons of war – tanks, guns, ships and aeroplanes. Some were retained, mothballed in case they should be required again but much of the weaponry went to the scrap dealers in the immediate post-war years.

JACK CARRADICE

I should guess the scrapyards had a field day after the war – somebody undoubtedly made a fortune out of it. It had to happen, of course, all that steel needed to be re-cycled – we probably ended up cooking in pots and pans that had once been part of a tank or anti-aircraft gun or something.

I'll always remember the mothball fleets that they used to have moored in the rivers, all those old destroyers and corvettes that had once battled across the Atlantic. Some of them broke loose in a gale one winter, just after the war and went ashore close to the Ridge below my house. By the time the Admiralty people had arrived they'd been picked clean – piracy, it seemed, was still rife!

Laid up and waiting for breaking, the end is near for one of Britain's now obsolete destroyers.

BILL WILLIAMS

One place I was sent after the war was Llandow. The thing that struck me, when I got there, was field after field of four engine bombers, all ready to be written off. Lancaster bombers. I used to think that most of Bomber Command was parked there.

I was with this Auxiliary Squadron and as fast as I repaired one, they'd bend another. But the fields were full of these Lancasters – I'll always remember that.

By the time the 1940s drew to a close, the economic condition of Britain had improved, perhaps not to the extent that it would save the Labour Government but certainly enough to make people feel that fighting the war and dealing with the austerity of the post-war years had not been in vain. There was a feeling of security in the air.

MARCO CARINI

The police were always in the shop, particularly at night when it was shutting-up time. They'd be there for a couple of hours, chatting. Then they'd go off on their rounds. Within an hour of them leaving the shop you'd hear them trying the door, trying the doors as they went down the road. It isn't done these days, the police are all in patrol cars now.

Marco Carini (right) with his mother, Angela, and brother Luigi.

VALERIE CARINI

My aunty had a shop and she always told us this story. She was in bed one night and a light from a torch came into the room. A policeman's voice said 'You've forgotten to lock your door.' Imagine that. The police always went around checking on the doors in the night.

As the 1940s ended, a degree of prosperity finally returned to the country – it was the start of a period where, as a future Prime Minister was later to say, 'You never had it so good.'

In many respects, surviving the post-war years of austerity had been harder than fighting the war. The enemy was not so easy to identify and progress was slower and more fraught with difficulty.

Yet it was a period that had to be endured and battled through, just like the years of conflict that had preceded it. Change came slowly – the children of the 1940s, for example, played much the same games as the children of the 1950s and 1960s. Entertainment and clothing did not alter very much, at least not until the revolutionary 1960s. Rationing ended but the young men of Britain remained in uniform as National Service, the Korean War, and the need to maintain a barrier against Russian incursion into Europe, demanded a standing army of considerable size and strength.

Luxury goods did start to appear in shops and wages did slowly increase. It was slow progress and many people wondered if all the effort had been worth it – at least for a while.

Yet without the years of austerity, Britain would not have been able to re-establish herself as an economically-viable community. Looking back now, and remembering that hindsight truly is the only exact science, many people can be excused for using Harold Macmillan's famous phrase – out of time and out of context, admittedly – and thinking to themselves 'You never had it so good.'

BIBLIOGRAPHY

A Cardiff Family in the Forties, Malcolm Pill, Merton Priory Press 1999

A History of Wales, John Davies, Penguin 1994

Chronology of World War Two, Edward Davidson & Dale Manning, Cassell & Co 1999

Great Contemporaries, Winston S Churchill, Fontana 1959

Landmarks in the History of Education, T L Jarman, John Murray 1963

National Coal Board: The First Ten Years, Anon, Colliery Guardian Co 1957

Never Again, Peter Hennessy, Vintage 1993

The Call Up, Tom Hickman, Headline 2004

The Fifties, Gareth Thomas, Parragon 2003

Under Siege, Robert Hewison, Weidenfeld & Nicholson 1977

Wales at War, Phil Carradice, Gomer 2003

Welcome Home, Ben Wicks, Bloomsbury Publishing 1991

Gomer and the Second World War

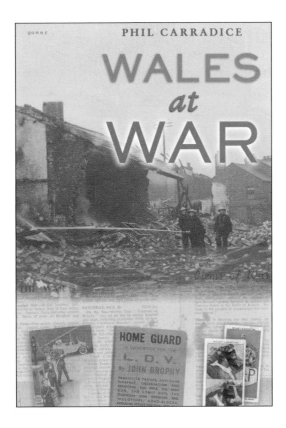

This book tells the stories of those men and women who never appear in the history textbooks. *Wales at War* gives voice to ordinary Welsh people who lived through the Second World War, and who have quite extraordinary stories to relate. Factory workers, Land Army girls, air-raid wardens, evacuees, firemen, prisoners of war, conscientious objectors, servicemen: all of these people have memories of particular intensity. Their readiness to share their experiences with author Phil Carradice has led to a book that is rich in detail and absolutely authentic in the attitudes and emotions it contains.

ISBN 1 84323 321 5   £9.99

Gomer and the Second World War

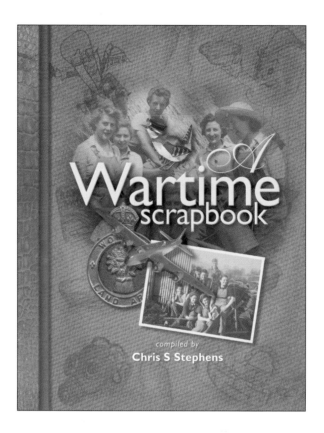

'Being a war baby was just hard luck' – or was it? Children growing up in wartime were certainly kept busy. They could be building a shelter, Digging for Victory in an allotment, taking a day off school for potato-picking, even befriending an evacuee. They had tasks to do – because many fathers were away at war and mothers working in weapons factories or perhaps driving lorries.

A Wartime Scrapbook will give children of the twenty-first century a vivid picture of the Second World War. It is a book for whole families to explore together, especially if grandparents or elderly relatives have memories of their own to share.

Chris Stephens, author of the popular anthologies *A Christmas Box* and *A Seaside Treat*, once again brings social history to life for readers of all ages.

Softback ISBN 1 84323 285 5   £5.99
Hardback ISBN 1 84323 390 8   £8.99

Gomer and the Second World War

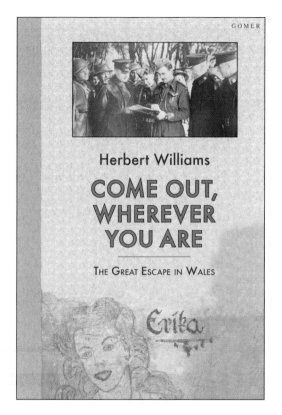

'This is the most forgotten story of the Second World War'

Byron Rogers

This is the true story of the Great Escape in Wales.
Forget the films and the fiction. This was the real thing. In March 1945,
67 German prisoners of war were on the run! Their daring escape from a
camp in Bridgend, South Wales, led to a massive manhunt involving
thousands of troops, police and civilians. Even Boy Scouts and Girl Guides
joined in the chase. It was a time of fear and panic.
Read all about it: in the words of those who took centre-stage, also in
press-clippings and the new and archive photographs that accompany this
breathless account of bravado and bravery, of folly and failure on both sides.

'A tremendous read'

Trevor Fishlock

ISBN 1 84323 199 9   £7.99